THE PROFESSIONAL CODE OF CONDUCT

THE PROFESSIONAL CODE OF CONDUCT

"Corporate America and How to Obtain Your Dream Internship or Job."

Michael J. Bottaro
Temple University Alumni—
Class of 2006

iUniverse, Inc.
New York Lincoln Shanghai

The Professional Code of Conduct
"Corporate America and How to Obtain Your Dream Internship or Job."

iUniverse books may be ordered through booksellers or by contacting:

iUniverse
2021 Pine Lake Road, Suite 100
Lincoln, NE 68512
www.iuniverse.com
1-800-Authors (1-800-288-4677)

Because of the dynamic nature of the Internet, any Web addresses or links contained in this book may have changed since publication and may no longer be valid.

The views expressed in this work are solely those of the author and do not necessarily reflect the views of the publisher, and the publisher hereby disclaims any responsibility for them.

ISBN: 978-0-595-46890-4 (pbk)
ISBN: 978-0-595-91179-0 (ebk)

Printed in the United States of America

Special Thanks

This book is dedicated to all the people who have been my mentors and inspirations to write this book. My passion has always been to help others, which was my goal when I began writing this book. I hope to help and touch the lives of as many people as possible who read this book and are pursuing the career of their dreams all across the country. I receive no other greater self-accomplishment than when I can make a contribution to the success of others. In my experiences I have been extremely fortunate enough to benefit from both my family and professional contacts that have been there to guide me throughout my entire career. I am led to believe that success is derived from observing and learning from others. I have learned a great deal from the contacts I have encountered over the course of my life and this is why I would like to share my experiences with my readers so that they can benefit as I have.

I would like to thank my parents first and foremost. Both my mother and father have always been there to support me and guide me throughout my professional endeavors. Also I would like to thank my brother Andrew who has always been supportive along with the rest of my family. A special thank you to Temple University who has provided me with all the essential tools needed for life after school in the corporate world of finance. The Center for Student Professional Development (CSPD) at Temple University was able to help me begin my career search in the past. The Financial Management Association (FMA), including my co-officers, students, and faculty were able to help me master professional conduct and the knowledge one could not receive in a classroom. Thank you to all my former employers and internship co-workers who were able to contribute to my career's start. The experience I was able to gain will never be forgotten. Also, I wanted to thank my friends who have been there to support me throughout my time as a student at Temple University, my career in financial advising and while writing this book. Without you all, this book would not have been made possible. Thank you.

Most sincerely,
Michael J. Bottaro

Contents

Introduction

Each year millions of college students and college graduates all over America take part in their internship and job searching process. Stressful? Of course. Applying for jobs and the interviewing process can be one of the most stressful times in a college student's life. Even the brightest students with the highest G.P.A.s are challenged with obtaining the job which they desire. One may be surprised, but sometimes the students with the highest G.P.A.s actually have the most difficulty obtaining jobs. This is why I am writing this book. My goal as an author is to pave the path for students all over America towards obtaining their dream jobs and internships.

I tend to think students are actually smarter than people give them credit for, however the majority of this intellect is often emphasized towards classroom knowledge and it is not applied towards professionalism in corporate America. This is where this book comes into play. This book is geared typically towards business majors, however I feel the book will still greatly benefit any college graduate or student approaching graduation in the near future. This book will correlate a little closer towards business students only because it is based on my personal experiences as a proud alumni from Temple University's Fox School of Business which was not only able to provide me with an excellent education, but provided several organizations and career centers which I took advantage of and allowed me to greatly enhance my professional career.

Grades are extremely important, however one of the greatest misconceptions of students and their parents is that grades are everything. This is far from the truth. Professionalism is everything in the society in which we live. If you do not possess the art of professionalism in the corporate world, you have nothing.

professional· [pr*uh*-**fesh**-*uh*-nl-iz-*uh* m]—*noun*
1. professional character, spirit, or methods.
2. the standing, practice, or methods of a professional, as distinguished from an ama-teur.

Notice, in the definition shown above "distinguished from amateur." You are indeed an amateur to the workforce when you are graduating with a bachelor's degree, however this is why it is crucial to make an employer aware of the strengths which you possess and how you have went above and beyond throughout college to better your experience and enhance the tools which you have obtained in a college classroom. Remember, in order to obtain your dreams, you can never settle for doing only what is expected or the bare minimum required. One of my points I am trying to make in writing this book is to allow others to know that you do not have to obtain straight A's to earn a job on Wall Street or for a Fortune 500 Company. Often receiving a job offer is based mainly on the way you present (sell) yourself and having a solid background of the company which you are interviewing with. When an employer realizes that you have a sound understanding of the company he/she works for, often the person interviewing will be impressed and you will already be one step ahead of half the candidates who are applying for the position which you are applying for. It is surprising how many candidates actually do not do their research on a company before entering an interview.

If you are already stressed, calm down. This book will provide 8 detailed chapters which will provide you with all the knowledge you will need towards obtaining your dream job. This is a book of professionalism, however you will find in the readings that my advice is portrayed in a matter which is quick to the point. We will even try to have a little fun in the book as I will add some light humor which I have experienced in the corporate world.

The Professional Code of Conduct will help prepare you with everything from what attire is considered suitable to wear in the business world to nailing an interview with an employer at the company of your dreams. The key in order to be successful at this is "balance." In order to be successful and have a great balance of strengths you need to make sure that you have enhanced all the professional attributes which an employer will be looking for in its candidates. Yes, grades are important, but you will also need to have a solid resume in a format which is considered no less than professional grade. Also, it is important to remain calm and be confident. Aside from possessing these qualities you will also need to be prepared for the curve balls which an employer will throw at you including trick questions and case studies which we will touch upon later in the book. They are the more advanced topics, so for now let's stick with the basics.

Finally, money and starting salaries are important, however it is not everything. I know you probably have all heard this before but it is the truth. In order to be happy, you must be happy with the field and area of work in which you are working in. You are dedicating at least 40 hours a week of your life to your career. If you are not happy during the hours you are at work, then you can bet that you will not be happy when you come home at night either. Besides salary, things you should always consider is the job's qualifications, scope of work, expectations and hours. You want to make sure that the skills and attributes the company values most match the qualities which you posses. For some people hours are an important factor due to their marital status and being able to obtain a healthy work/life balance.

Everything we have just talked about and much more will be discussed in thorough detail going forward. You may want to even take notes so that you do not forget the most important things that you will take away from this book. Ok, so now you at least know what professionalism is and why it is important. Now it is time to learn how you can enhance these vital skills of professionalism and become far better prepared than your competition when interviewing for a job.

CHAPTER 1

Four Crucial Skills in the Corporate World

In order to become successful in the corporate business world, four skills are crucial to obtain upon graduation. These four skills include COMMUNICATIONS, LEADERSHIP, TEAMWORK and QUANITATIVE ANALYSIS. The first step towards success includes possessing these four traits. Not only is it important to obtain these skills, but it is important to mention them in an interview by using specific examples as how you have demonstrated use of each of these four skills.

Employers at every elite company desire to find a candidate who possesses a balance of all four of these characteristics. Ok great, the secret is out. You know the four skills which an employer is looking for but you are still not even half of the way there. Now the tough part comes into play, how do you prove to an employer that you posses each of these skills? Your next question may be to ask how I can convince an employer that I have these skills.

As a college student nearly all enrolled students have the ability and access to the resources to acquire these traits. However if you wish to reach your goals, it requires doing more than what is expected. Also the old saying of "practice makes perfect" definitely applies. For example, if you know that you lack communication skills, practice them by volunteering to present a project or case study in front of your professor and classmates.

Employers realize as a new hire out of college that your work experience is limited and that you have not mastered each of these four traits. However, it is important to prove to the employer interviewing you that you have taken time out of your busy schedule to improve your knowledge and experience in each of these categories. What you will find is it is actually a lot simpler than you may think to improve your skills in each of these categories.

First and foremost, communications are crucial in the business world in which we work today. In my opinion this is the most important trait to master because every other trait feeds off this skill. If you can or have mastered this skill, everything else discussed in this book will easily come into play and you will be quickly on your way toward reaching your goals and success. To be an excellent communicator you need to be comfortable with people, remain relaxed at all time, express that you are confident, think quick on your feet, and do not show anger even if difficult situations arise. Communications can be enhanced by presenting a project in front of your professor and classmates or even just your parents if the opportunity does not arise from the classroom. Remember, whenever you are called to present to a group or an individual it is important that you fully understand the subject or material which you are talking to your peers and/or co-workers about. This can often be accomplished by asking "good" questions. If you do not understand something, ask the question. It is more important to fully understand a problem you are having than to ignore it. In the long run you will find the value of this technique. There really is no such thing as a dumb question. If you do not ask questions you will not know how to respond to the question and fix the problem when you are called to answer it in the future.

A good rule of thumb for any good communicator before presenting to a group is using the "Grandmom" technique. When I use this term, I am referring to the importance of explaining material in a clear and thorough fashion so that even if you had to explain your presentation to your grandmother, she would be able to understand everything which you have just presented. You have to realize when you present to others, even people of high level positions and educational backgrounds, they may not be familiar with the particular job which you hold or have held. This is why it is important that you explain all points in detail. You always have to expect that your audience is not familiar with the material which you are conveying.

Communication also involves more than just words. It is important to use good hand gestures and voice tones when you are talking with others or are called to present. For example, if you present while keeping your hands in your pockets or shaking with a laser pointer in your hand, not only are you most likely uncomfortable but so is your audience to which you are presenting.

Remember, stay loose and relax. It is only a presentation. If you know your material and have asked all the questions needed before you present everything should be fine. Presentations are something that will become easier for one with practice over time. Every presentation I have given, no matter what topic is has been, has become easier over time.

As part of the job interview process, you may be asked to make a presentation. In this case you are taking part in the act of "selling" yourself. Often you will find these styles of interviewing common when applying for positions in financial advising because it is the career in business which is one of most important in terms of possessing excellent communication skills. If you can not communicate with others and sell your product your career in the industry will be extremely short lived.

Technology has also created another sector of communication practice which exists in our current society. One must remember, due to the advances of technology such as the internet, e-mail is a crucial form of communication. Even though my other examples were verbal forms of communication, it is still important to take writing skills into consideration. These skills include careful communication and grammar. Before sending an e-mail, always double and triple check that the recipient is the correct intended contact. In the corporate world you will be asked to send confidential documents and information so it is important to find its proper recipients and to keep out of the hands of others. Also, before sending your document, make sure that you spell check your e-mail. Poor spelling really looks unprofessional when you send an e-mail. As a word of advice, almost all e-mail accounts have an option which you can use allowing you to spell check your text before sending the e-mail. I would suggest you select this feature. Microsoft Outlook is the most common e-mail account system used in the corporate world which definitely has this option featured.

Leadership is another trait important to possess in order to become successful. Leadership includes taking responsibility for an important role and setting the perfect example for others. A person possessing good leadership skills will go out of his/her way to accomplish a task or doing more than is expected. Often, this may be the toughest of all tasks for one to obtain because it requires having a great deal of courage. As a leader it is also important to remember to be ethical and make a decision which is in the best interest of your company, clients, etc.

So you may ask as a college student, "How can I become a leader?" The answer is simple. Join a professional organization. They exist in all colleges and universities in nearly every major. If you are unsure how to join a professional organization you can always contact the dean's office in your university's school specific to your major. Also, becoming a leader does not only require joining the organization, but it requires a great deal of participating and working your way up to an officer position. After dedicating your time to your major study's organization, express you're interested in becoming an officer to an existing officer or faculty advisor if you have not already been approached to do so. By doing this, in the future when you are asked "Demonstrate how you have conducted yourself as a leader," the answer for you will be simple.

As finance major at Temple University I was the Executive Vice President of the Financial Management Association. Acquiring the position as Executive Vice President was not a quick or easy path. Obtaining the position required joining the organization as a sophomore and actively participating. Junior year I then expressed interest in becoming an officer and I was offered a position as the Vice President of Student Affairs where I was able to list job postings for our organization's members and help other students build their resumes and find internships. This position which I held, was the real inspiration for me to write this book. I always knew, based on the description of the position which I held, that it would be a great fit for me because it included my greatest passion as its major description, which was helping and remaining in close contact with the organization's members. I receive no greater thrill than to help others succeed. It is a very rewarding feeling when you impact other people's ability to succeed. I was then able to make the transition as an officer of a professional organization in college to a position as a financial advisor for an elite investment firm right out of college. You may not realize it in college, but when you finally receive your first job or internship, you will realize how big of an impact joining a professional organization had on obtaining the position.

By the time my senior year approached, I was then named the Executive Vice President of the Financial Management Association. I noticed the leadership responsibility which I held significantly increased at each level. The position definitely was able to prepare me for the real corporate world and I was able to receive a great feeling of self accomplishment. We were able to expand the organization's membership size, obtain increased funding, and receive the Superior Chapter Award for the 3rd straight year which I felt I had made a large contribution towards. The Superior Chapter Award signified that the Financial Management at Temple University was ranked in the top 5% of greatest accomplished Chapters in the entire country in terms of revenues and membership.

Remember, it is great to join a professional committee to enhance the knowledge that you cannot gain in a classroom and acquire an extra bullet point on your resume, but it is also important to gain all the value out of the organization you can possibly acquire. This involves working on a professional organization's committee and becoming an officer of the organization. This is your first real step towards becoming a leader and making an impact in corporate America which you will be soon entering in the near future.

Leadership is a crucial skill to possess in order to receive advancement in any company which one will work in corporate America. Employers and upper management will quickly notice strong leadership traits which their employees possess. Often leadership development is crucial because upper management is taking notice of those who have strong potential to one day become future managers within the corporation. By demonstrating strong leadership qualities you will find yourself one step ahead of your co-workers when pursuing a management position in the future.

The third skill important to possess in the business world is the art of teamwork. Teamwork is crucial in order for any successful business team to work. In any corporate job you will be called to apply this skill as well, so it is important that you demonstrate that you possess this trait in an interview. Besides group projects, which you will be asked to participate in your classes throughout the time spent in college, there are plenty of other techniques where you can enhance your teamwork skills.

Teamwork requires taking the initiative to work with others in an orderly fashion to complete a project or accomplish a goal. Teamwork often requires not only pitching in your portion of work, but it requires the ability to delegate work to others. When delegating work to others keep in mind it is important to recognize your peers or co-workers' strengths so that you can delegate work which will complete the project in the most efficient manner.

Often one may find it difficult to enhance their teamwork skills if they are not given the opportunity. In the case of a college student, this is why it is so important to join a professional organization. As an officer of a professional organization you will be called upon to work with your team of officers. You will have several projects that need to be completed with the input of all officers' collaborated thoughts, ideas and hard work. It is important to always remain open to all of your peers' opinions. By doing so, teamwork will work most efficiently.

If one is a college graduate and no longer has the opportunity to join a professional committee, do not worry. There are plenty of other ways you can enhance you teamwork skills. One can enhance their teamwork skills by taking the initiative to assist in organizing a community service or charity event. By taking part in such an event, one will be able to work with plenty of other members of the community as a team with the goal of completing a project for a good cause. Employers will take notice that you are a hard working person who took time out his/her busy schedule to make a difference and contribute towards a great cause. When one participates in a community service event, it sends a message to an employer that you care about the work that you do and also that you have good work ethics. Teamwork is a powerful skill to possess. By proving to an employer that you can work effectively with others towards reaching a desired goal, you will find yourself much more marketable in the hire selection process.

Finally, quantitative/analytical skills are one of the most desired skills which an individual needs to possess in order to be successful in the business field. This is true especially as an accounting, finance or risk management major. Quantitative skills are so crucial to have a solid understanding of because often in one's career as a business professional you will be called to make sound financial decisions which require a strong understanding of algebra and accounting. Hopefully for a business major, this should be one of the easier skills to grasp. This skill is the trait which correlates closest with the classroom material which a student has covered, opposed to the previous three skills which relate closer to outside classroom activities and jobs.

One will often find that in an interview when an employer is interested in learning about your quantitative skills he/she will not necessarily ask you what quantitative skills you possess, however you may be asked to calculate something off the top of your head on the spot. Stressful? Yes, it can be. Even if you are incredible at mathematics, interviews can definitely be stressful and that is why even the simplest of math problems may be difficult to answer on the spot. Keep in mind this is doing basic math in your head. NO CALCULATOR! You will need to then think fast and come up with an answer to their "on the spot" question. Most employers will not give you a problem which is impossible to answer in your head. This is simply a test of your basic math skills, logic and problem solving under a stressful situation. Remain calm and you will be fine.

You may ask what an employer could ask you regarding mathematics in an interview. For example, you may be asked on an interview with an investment firm, "If we have a client base of 20,000 served by 50 advisors here, what is the client/advisor ratio?" This is a good example of what may be asked. In fact, I have indeed been asked this exact question at an interview before. You probably already know the answer to this problem, however we will save answering questions like these and more difficult questions which are often asked by employers for later in my book. More quantitative problems will be practiced in the chapters when we discuss trick interview questions. It is important to have a solid understanding of the basic professional codes first before we move onto the more advanced material.

Quantitative/analytical skills can be enhanced by practicing problems in textbooks, buying online tutorials and pursuing graduate school programs. These are all great sources, however they are not the only valuable sources available either. Even sitting with a few friends or co-workers to discuss the stock market in a casual manner can be effective. You may want to take a few minutes out of your day to determine which stocks appear to be profitable over the short and long term without using the given stock rating provided on websites, for example MSN. Remember, sometimes the market is wrong in their valuations. Not often, but this will occur from time to time. You can maintain your sharp quantitative skills by calculating the ratios manually which any advanced investor would use to make a financial decision as to buy or sell the stock. Such ratios would include calculating formulas such as P.E. (Price/Earnings) Ratio, E.P.S. (Earnings per Share) Ratio, and Dividend Yield.

If quantitative skills are a trait which you need to improve upon I would recommend doing basic math in your head. Basic math may even include using large numbers into the millions by doing basic multiplication and division to calculate ratios. This may seem insulting advice to finance or accounting majors who frequently have to do computations such as these. Regardless, these computations are important for business majors to be able to calculate in order to make important business decisions. The old saying stays true, "Practice does make perfect."

When applying for your next job in your job search and interviewing with employers make sure you keep these four characteristics in mind. Every employer is looking for these four skills so make sure that you possess solid balance of these skills and you can convince an employer that you possess them as well. These four skills should indeed be easy to be identified by employers on both your resume and while interviewing. Both are important because first you need to be chosen in the selection process for an interview by creating a one page document of your greatest skills and accomplishments. Once selected for an interview, the second part is mastering the interview process in an one on one meeting with the employer. This is the part where you need to "sell" yourself. Regardless what your major area of study is in school, you need to have a basic understanding of marketing to be offered the job position you are applying for.

As an employer, you are looking for your candidate to be the answer or solution to your company's problem(s). When applying to a Fortune 500 Company, such as G.E., Johnson & Johnson, Merrill Lynch, Citigroup, JP Morgan Chase, I.B.M., etc. it is important to keep in mind that there are thousands of people who apply for positions at each of these firms every year with only a limited amount of open positions in existence. So what separates you from all the rest? Answer: Possessing these four skills is a nice start. Second is practicing and mastering them. When an employer receives tens of thousands of resumes each year, their thought process is not how to hire you, but how to eliminate you. Your resume often goes through a computer filtration process before even being read by human eyes. So how do you get your resume to the top of the pile? We will save that for our next chapter where I will answer your questions on creating the prefect resume. Now that you have a strong understanding of the four most important professional skills, it is time to move on so that you can learn about creating your resume using these four skills and begin being recognized.

CHAPTER 2

Establishing a Flawless Resume

Establishing a flawless resume is probably the sole most important professional quality needed to possess in order to be successful. Your resume is your employers' first impression of you. Your resume is pure marketing. In order to compile a successful resume, you must be able to market yourself effectively in one typed page or less.

Remember, employers do not want your life's history included. Always sell yourself thoroughly in the most concise way possible. Employers receive thousands and thousands of resumes each year. Many will not even be read. One full page is plenty of information for a student who is just finishing school. Depending on your qualifications and job experience a second page could be included if used appropriately. I would only recommend using a second page after you now have a few years of real world experience under your belt. Regardless, two pages should always be the maximum length for your resume.

My goal in this chapter is to have your resume recognized and placed on top of the pile. Always research and do your homework on the company which you are applying to as well. You want to modify your resume for each employer so that you can add or change skills and "buzz words" on your resume so that you become the solution to the employer's problem at the company to which you are applying. If you do not possess these qualifications or traits desired by an employer, your resume goes straight to the trash can. This chapter will be able to help you establish a well developed resume so that it will include everything which an employer searches for in the most professional manner. (We will discuss buzz words later in this chapter along with their importance in the early stages of your job search process.)

To start with the basics, first and foremost, always make sure your resume includes your name and contact information at the very top of the paper. A standard resume should also be in Times New Roman 11 size font. For an entry level position your resume should be one page in length at most. An employer realizes that you are still an amateur in your field of study. You are applying for an entry level position out of college so it is important for your resume to be concise and as informative as possible without being too wordy. Always make sure that your resume is laid out neatly using bullet-points and correct spacing. Spelling is also crucial. Nothing is more horrible to see than a resume with misspelled words and incorrect grammar. If an employer notices this, your resume will be the first paper ball slam dunked into the waste basket.

A word of advice, have a friend, family member and a professional contact such as a teacher or co-worker review and spell check your resume before submitting it to an employer for the first time. It is always a good idea to have several people review it because each person who reviews it may find a different correction to make which the other may have missed. Remember Spell Check in Microsoft Office does not always catch every error. This is why extra measures are needed to be taken in order to be certain you have established a flawless resume. Also, if your school has a professional development center, it would be an excellent idea for them to review your resume as well. This would probably be your most effective source. Some schools may even require this process if you are using their services to search for a job or internship.

Aside from the vital contact information at the very top and making sure you have spelled everything correctly, your resume's content and choice of "buzz words" are also crucial. The buzz words may even be the single most important aspect of your resume. Your resume's content should always include your education information, work history and skills. In your resume you should include your date of graduation or expected date of graduation along with the school you attend. Always include your field(s) of study. Underneath the previous information, optional details you may want to include are your G.P.A and semesters in which you made the dean's list (if applicable).

Lastly, and definitely most importantly, I can not stress enough to include what professional organization you joined along with the positions which you held. Even if you only take one thing away from this entire book, please remember the importance of joining a professional committee. Make sure this is included in your resume. If you have not joined a professional committee yet, now is the time to join. Also, make sure you actively participate and strive to apply for officer positions. Every college and university, big or small in size, has these organizations at their school.

Organizations may market their club to get students to join and you often may think it is just another learning event or meeting where if I sit and listen to the organization's presentation I can get a free pizza lunch or something, which is usually how the organizations advertise. These are typical students' impressions of these organizations. Some students join just for the mere fact of obtaining a resume bullet point. To be honest, I suppose a bullet point is better than nothing, however you are paying a membership fee which is usually included. Why not take full advantage of your money? If you can actively participate and become an organization officer such as a president, vice-president, treasurer, secretary or committee member you will be that much more prepared to start your career than most other college students.

Also, what your school and these organizations don't tell you is that this is the beginning of your career. Sure you don't get paid for it, but money isn't everything, especially early in your career, when your main goal should be becoming well rounded and becoming acquainted with corporate America and its atmosphere. As a college student, you should take in as much information as possible in a relaxed atmosphere, such as a professional organization, so that you develop and grow much quicker in your future career. Again, take my advice, pay your $75 annual fee or whatever the cost may be and I can assure you that you will not regret it. The knowledge you will gain will always remain with you throughout all levels in your career. Throughout your life many things can be taken from you. Your knowledge and experiences can never be taken. After all is said and done you may agree that this has been the most well spent money you can remember in your life.

Why again should an employer hire you? The answer is your skills, experience and work history are a good start. First you should include your skills which are most specific to the company to which you are applying. Remember, your resume is answering the employer's question of how can this applicant affect our firm. Always ask yourself those types of questions first and foremost before clicking that submit resume button on CareerBuilder.com or other websites which you may use to submit your resume to employers. Also when including these skills or traits you possess, be prepared to explain to an employer and give specific examples of times you demonstrated these skills. Do not worry too much about giving specific examples at the moment. We will discuss this more in detail later in the book when we begin to discuss interviewing skills. Even though we haven't discussed the interviewing skills yet when asked to describe your skills, it is important to include evidence of these skills for your employer by describing them indirectly in your work history.

Always be honest in your resume. Never overstate your strengths. If you are putting in the extra effort to read this book, I am sure you are intelligent enough to realize you already possess many strengths. Don't add others skills which are not strengths just to list them. State what your strengths are because if you include a skill or trait which is not a strength of yours, you will not be comfortable to talk about it when you are asked about it later down the line. Remember, there is nearly always a way you can position previous experience to the job in which you are applying. It just takes practice to perfect this skill of convincing an employer you have what it takes to be successful working at their firm.

There will also be a time in almost all interviews where you will be asked, "What are your weaknesses?" That would be the time to include a skill or two in which you are not comfortable, however, of course you are going to want to position it to an employer in a manner where you can bring a positive feature out of such a question. Again, we will discuss this in more detail later in this book.

The skills you will describe are not only the four major skills employers search for but also other adjectives which describe your work ethics and strengths. These types of skills should be listed throughout your entire resume. It is important to include programs, certifications, awards and language skills you possess as well. It is also important to position them in a job specific manner. For example, if you are applying for a financial analyst or accounting position at Johnson & Johnson, you may want to specify that you have solid Microsoft Office skills and three years experience in SAP software. However, if you are applying for a position at an investment firm such as Merrill Lynch, you may want to specify that you are NASD Series 6 and 63 certified and can speak Spanish which may be applicable to dealing with clients who speak only Spanish. Generally you will include specific skills at the bottom of your resume which you will title "Skills" or "Skills and Languages."

When stating your work experience, always list the most recent employer first with two or three bullet points under each employer. For the next one or two employers, state the jobs you held which are most relevant to the new job for which you are applying. Remember, each employer is looking for something different. Modification is important for each employer. Even if you only have two or three resumes created, it is still more effective than having one. If you are a finance major it would probably be recommended to make at least two. You would want to create one for a financial advisor position and one for an analyst/accountant position. If floor trading or auditing are also of interest maybe you would want to have a total of three or four resumes created.

Remember when citing your previous employers, ask yourself the questions, "Why would this employer want to hire me?" and "How can I prove to this employer that I can effectively contribute to their firm?" These are the types of questions you need to ask yourself, be able to answer, and then effectively put into words on your one page resume.

"Buzz words" are a crucial aspect, which needs to be included in any flawless resume. This may be the part of the resume which students and applicants are most unfamiliar with and yet it may be possibly the most important. Without these buzz words included in your resume, it may never be even looked at or read. This is step one in the job search process. If you can not get beyond step one, the following steps are useless. This is why this chapter will be heavily weighted on this point.

Each year employers receive several thousands of resumes. In reality even the largest firms can only hire a couple hundred people, if even that many. When an employer receives such a large volume of resumes they may not even get a chance to read your resume. Often employers have a computer screening process. If your resume doesn't even include any of these buzz words, your resume is instantaneous deleted. This is why it is so important to include these buzz words in your resume. I can assure you, whether you obtain the job you are applying for or not, you have already greatly enhanced the chances of you receiving a phone call for an interview date if your resume includes the buzz words.

I have provided a list of buzz words essential when applying to a corporate job. (These may also be applicable to other fields as well depending on what job you are applying for.)

Resume Buzz Words

Administered	Advised	Analyzed	Assembled
Assisted	Collaborated	Complied	Conducted
Conveyed	Coordinated	Created	Cultivated
Developed	Ensured	Facilitated	Gathered
Generated	Implemented	Instructed	Interviewed

Led	Licensed	Maintained	Managed
Mentored	Organized	Oversaw	Planned
Presented	Processed	Promoted	Reconciled
Researched	Screened	Shadowed	Solicited
Supervised	Surveyed	Tallied	Taught
Tracked			

Other Resume Buzz Words and Phrases

Achievement of business goals	Achievement of sales goals
Conflict resolute	Cost analysis
Cost efficiency	Due diligence
Ensuring customer satisfaction	Liaison
Managed day-to-day operations	Managing client relationships
Meeting client needs	Problem solving
Process improvement	Supervised logistics
Team Leader	

A completed resume should contain a good balance of all these traits I have mentioned. Once you have included all of these in your resume you have completed the first step towards obtaining your dream internship or job and are on your way towards corporate success. A resume can be described best as the document you produce where you can best sell yourself to an employer. Remember to keep your resume short and sweet. You should include all your greatest strengths and most relevant work and school experiences. If you take your time while creating your resume and include all the points in this book, I guarantee you will be contacted by many more employers than you had been previous to reading this book.

Cover letters may also be asked by employers to be included. My advice is if they are not mandatory, omit them from your application. Cover letters are extra information which is not an accurate reflection of your job qualifications and performance. If an employer does make it mandatory to include a cover letter I would advice creating a professional letter in business format. Cover letters should almost be specifically customized to a particular employer's needs. This is why if it is not necessary, I would not include a cover letter. Cover letters are very time consuming and if you wish to apply to several firms, you may be rushing through creating them and it could hinder your chances of getting hired instead of helping your chances.

When creating a cover letter, always make sure to state your skills, specific examples and why you would make an excellent fit for the position. What an employer really wants to know is why should I hire this candidate and how can this employee effectively contribute to our company's performance?

My final tip for you is to complete the resume process and send it to employers early in your college years. The sooner you can send your resume to employers the better off your career will progress. A common misconception of college students is that internships are not attainable until after your junior year. As a student graduating college, it is true that the experience you have is limited, however, this is why it is important that you gather as much experience as possible in the time you did attend college. Employers will take careful notice to this experience. Grades are important as well, however they are by far not the most important factor in an interviewer's decision. Almost all employers will even admit this to you. I have seen students in the past with a 2.8 G.P.A. obtain an incredible job after school over the student with the 3.8 G.P.A. because the student with the 2.8 G.P.A had done internships in his college years, while the student with the 3.8 G.P.A. had no job experience.

Now that you have what it takes to create a flawless resume, our next step is how to present yourself and interact with employers once you receive a call from them or meet with a representative at a job fair, open house, interview, etc.

(I have included an example of what your resume should look like once it is completed. The resume I have included is a resume similar to the one I created as a senior undergrad student at Temple University pursuing a career in the world of finance.)

<u>**JOE PROSPEROUS**</u>   *e-mail: jprosperous@temple.edu*
123 Studious Drive | Philadelphia | PA | 19152 | tel: 215.555.0122

OBJECTIVE: To obtain an entry level position in a financial firm where I can contribute effectively as a leader to obtain corporate success.

EDUCATION: TEMPLE UNIVERSITY, Fox School of Business & Management, Philadelphia, PA
Bachelor of Business Administration, Graduation: May 2008
Major: Finance & Real Estate
GPA: 3.20

ACTIVITIES & AWARDS:

Financial Management Association, FMA, 2004-present

- Executive Vice President, 2006-2007

- Director of Student Professional Progression, 2005-2006

- Volunteer, Red Cross Help Line for Hurricane Katrina Victims, 2005

- Dean's List, Fall 2005

- Top ranked participant, FMA Stock Market Competition, 2004

EXPERIENCE: ARS INSTITUTE, Malvern, PA   May 2007–September 2007

Accounting/Finance Intern

- Processing invoices for a client base of more than 20,000 in the promotional products industry.

- Generate firm's account receivable memos by compiling tax and shipping data of all sales shipped world-wide for its daily operations.

THOMAS FAMOUS SEAFOOD,   October 2001–May 2007
Philadelphia, PA

Assistant Manager

- Supervise daily operations with more than 40 employees for wholesale operation specializing in pre-cooked seafood distribution to supermarkets.

- Maintain inventory, process orders, ensure sanitation of machinery, and oversee facility security for 16,000 sq. foot processing plant.

- Manage day to day operations for product loading and transit, and processing plant sanitation.

BUCKS COUNTY SWIM CLUB,   March 2001–May 2004
Richboro, PA

Maintenance Supervisor

- Ensured cleanliness of an upscale private swim club with 4,000+ members.

- Compiled together a strong maintenance crew of 10 whom with myself, maintained a healthy club atmosphere.

- Led maintenance crew and created a greatly respected image, receiving frequent positive feedback of members.

SKILLS & LANGUAGES:

- MS Office Suite

- Real Estate investing

- Spanish, reading, speaking

CHAPTER 3

Professional Attire

First impressions are everything. Appearance and professional attire are the proof of this statement. An individual who wishes to be treated like a professional must also dress like one in order to be well respected. When meeting with an employer for the first time, he/she will take notice of everything from you haircut to your shoes. Dress to impress is the key. If you are ever uncertain which wardrobe to wear or hair style to have, always choose the most conservative choice. It never can hurt to be too conservative. This rule is especially true for a first interview with an employer.

Is a wardrobe or hair cut the most fair way to judge a person applying for a job at your firm? Probably not and it definitely is not the best indicator of who is best qualified for the position, however life is not always fair in the world in which we live. What we have to do is to live by these values and the professional code of conduct. This will insure that we do not make any decisions which could possibly decrease our chances on being hired by an employer of our choice.

This chapter may seem rather obvious, however I still believe it is essential to cover all areas of professionalism in corporate America. Even if you just pick up on one or two little details which you didn't know previously to reading this chapter, then in my mind it has been a success.

Ok, so the phone rings. Congratulations on receiving your first scheduled interview. Now the next question is what should I wear? For men, there should not be a doubt in your mind that a suit is the only suitable choice. Even if you have a friend who works for the company and indicates that the company's dress code policy is business casual, you still want to dress your best the first time you meet with an employer. We will discuss later in the chapter what defines business casual, however for now we will stick strictly to what is appropriate to wear for interviews, job fairs, and formal business dinners.

A suit is always a requirement for men. If you leave the suit home you can almost forget being hired. No one ever said you have to buy a $2000 Armani suit. You just need to wear something presentable. You can get by just owning one suit, especially if it is not required to be worn once you start working for the company. A $200 suit from the Men's Warehouse or a store like that should serve your purpose perfectly. No one ever said you need to look like a million bucks, just presentable enough to be hired. Once you get hired and feel the need to look like a million bucks you can go ahead and do so after you are making big money.

For a first interview always wear a dark or neutral color suit. Do not wear any bright colors or something which will become blinding and a distraction to an interviewer. I would refrain from wearing a red, pink, yellow or other bright color you would see on an actor's suit in a movie. I would only recommend three suit colors for an interview. Navy blue, black, or gray would look presentable. In my opinion navy blue would actually be the best choice of all. If you wish to purchase a pin stripe suit that would be fine as well, however do not wear a suit where the lines are too bold. A standard thin line pin stripe suit would certainly be an appropriate form of attire for an interview.

Underneath your suit I would recommend wearing a white shirt with a solid color tie. Again, do not wear anything too bright or eye distracting. The best combination for shirt and tie in my opinion would be the presidential look. If you do not know what the presidential look is, it is a white shirt with a red tie. Do not buy a tie which is too bright in color. A standard crimson red would look great. Always make sure you wear a dark colored leather belt and a newly shined pair of dress shoes with dress socks.

For men, it is also appropriate to accessorize as long as it is not excessive. Remember dress to impress, but do not go over board either. Appropriate accessories would be a nice formal watch or small dress cufflinks. I would refrain however from wearing any form of earrings, gold bracelets or anything else which may seem like a distraction to an employer. There will be times where you will have to use your best judgment. Just always think back to my rule of conservativeness when in doubt and you will make the correct decision.

Finally for men, always take in consideration your hair style. Your hair should not be what is most trendy. This should also be a judgment call.

Acceptable forms of hair styles are a buzzed cut, comb over or even a shaved head. I would not advise long hair which falls to the shoulder, hair in a pony tail or spiked hair. Proper grooming and maintenance of facial hair is also important so that you have a nice clean look for when you meet with an employer. Unshaved facial hair often indicates poor organization skills or poor time management skills because it looks like you cannot find time to properly take care of yourself. An employer may often relate this to your work ethics. Again use your best judgment before leaving the house.

For women, this is a bit more difficult as what is business appropriate. The conservative theory will apply even more so to women than it did when discussing the men. The same colors apply to women as it did with men in terms of the choice of wardrobe. The most appropriate and conservative attire for women is the typical formal dress or a skirt suit. Again navy blue or black would probably be most appropriate. If you are going to wear a dress, women should always make sure that the dress is not too short. A good length is that a woman's dress should be no shorter than above her knees. Also, unless a woman's entire leg is covered, hosiery is required to be worn. Even if only the ankles are exposed a woman should still wear some form of stockings. If women do not feel comfortable wearing a dress, a woman's pant suit or blazer are also acceptable forms of attire. The same colors also apply for pant suits. If a woman chooses to wear a pant suit or blazer, a dress shirt should be worn underneath as well. Finally, for shoes women should always wear closed toe dress shoes, preferably heels if they want to take the most presentable and conservative approach. The shoes do not have to be high heels, however they should have some form of heel so that the attire meets its most professional status.

Accessories for women may include stud earrings, a necklace, watch, dark colored formal purse, or bracelets if not excessive. Women have a little more lenience here, however it is still important not to over accessorize. Earrings are indeed an acceptable form of accessory to be worn with their dress or suit, however I would refrain from wearing hoop or dangling earrings. A woman's handbag should always match the color of their shoes as well. Also women should avoid bright color nail polish on their nails and extreme make-up usage and colors. Just like men, women as well do not want to bring unnecessary attention to themselves. Although some hoop earrings may be acceptable, again use your best judgment to conservatism.

For men and women, always remember the rule of three for cologne. Especially in a formal interview, do not spray an excessive amount of cologne or perfume on yourself. Three squirts should be plenty. I actually have spoke with several employers over the years and have received this feedback repeatedly across the board. Many employers say that candidates over spray themselves. I am not saying do not wear cologne or perfume, however limit how much you actually spray on yourself. Remember, you are on a job interview and not on a date.

We have covered formal business attire, now it is time to discuss business casual attire. If your office's policy is considered business casual it does not literally mean casual. For men, business casual is actually pretty much the same thing as formal minus the suit jacket. Business casual for men is dress pants, slacks or khakis which will be worn with a dress shirt and tie. A nice pair of shined shoes, dress socks and a belt should be worn to complete the wardrobe. A sweater vest may also be considered a proper form of business casual attire as well.

Business causal for women is dress pants or skirts worn with a dress shirt or sweater. The same rules apply for their hosiery and accessories as well. Their choice of shoes however may be different. For business casual, heels do not have to be worn however the shoes worn by women still must be a formal form of closed-toe shoe.

This concludes the etiquette on how to dress when interviewing with an employer or how to dress once hired. Remember the two most important things which should be taken into consideration before you leave your home for an interview should be "conservatism" and "common sense." If you take these two points into consideration you will be well prepared to give a great first impression to the employer who is interviewing you.

Below I have provided a wardrobe chart which will break down what I have discussed for both men and women's attire for both business formal and business casual situations.

Business Formal Attire

Men	Women
-suit	-formal dress
-sport jacket	-pant suit
-dress pants	-blazer
-dress shirt	-dress shirt

Business Formal Attire

Men

-tie

-leather belt

-polished dress shoes

-dress socks

Women

-dress skirt

(not above knees)

-hosiery

-closed-toe heels

-handbag (if matches shoes)

Business Casual Attire

Men

-dress shirt

-tie

-sweater

-dress pants, khakis, slacks

-belt

-polished dress shoes

-dress socks

Women

-dress shirt

-sweater

-dress pants

-skirt

-blouse

-closed-toe dress

shoes

-handbag (if matches shoes)

CHAPTER 4

Networking Skills

Networking is one of the major keys in becoming successful in the corporate world of finance and almost all other fields. Networking is the structure and backbone of how most business is conducted. The definition of networking can be best described as:

net·work·ing [**net**-wur-king]—verb
To interact or engage in informal communication with others for mutual assistance or support.

Networking is the informal socializing with business associates, co-workers, employers, and their applicants. Even though networking may be considered informal, it is still important to remain professional. The socializing only remains informal in a sense that the discussions may not necessarily contain solely in-depth conversations about advanced work material and all work related topics. There are all types of networking as well. Networking may include career fairs, formal business dinners open to a target audience of professionals or college alumni students, or even dinners with your company whom you are employed by.

Networking is often a time aside from work where you can learn more about an employer's past experiences both at the firm you are applying to and previous to that firm. Networking is also another way an employer can learn more about you as well. As I stated before, even though this may be an informal event it is still important to make a good first impression and impress the person whom you are speaking with. For example, if you meet someone at a career fair and leave a good enough impression, he/she whom you are networking with may attempt to set up an interview with you or even offer you a job!

Recapping from Chapter 3, always dress professional at these events. Business casual at minimum, however if ever uncertain I would always recommend taking the most conservative approach and dress business formal. At any career fair, there should be no doubt in your mind that the attire is solely business formal. Again, you are looking to make a strong first impression. By wearing a suit, you can not lose.

At a career fair or recruiting dinner an employer's main goal is to recruit and find candidates who they think are qualified to be called into their firm's headquarters for an interview. Your job is to set yourself apart from the numerous other students who have walked up to their table to drop off a resume. What most students don't realize is that these career fairs are not simply just an event to drop off your resume and walk away. Yes, at a career fair the time you have to speak to an employer is limited. You may even be limited to just a few minutes with the employer, however, make the best use of these few minutes you do have. Taking a different approach then most students would is how you have to think. Your goal is you want to be remembered. Instead of trying to drop off a resume with all 90 or 100 employers who showed up for the fair, the better choice would be to pick 5 or 6 in which you have the most interest. Once you have selected 5 or 6 employers who best fit your career objectives, make sure you research and do your homework on each company so that you have a few well prepared topics for each employer that you plan to meet.

Most students I have met with over the years have expressed to me their frustration with these career fairs. They often approach me and say, "Mike, I dropped off resumes with nearly every employer in that auditorium and I still cannot seem to obtain a job or even receive a phone call for an interview." My next question to them is, "Of these 90 employers in attendance, how many did you actually have conversations with and have questions prepared for them which you asked?" The concept here is rather simple but most college students do not realize this. Dating back to our parents' age an individual may be able to use this excuse and want to meet with every employer. In our generation of modern day society with advanced technology and the internet at our fingertips, we have no excuses to not be able to send a resume to every firm we wish to apply to. To drop your resume off to each employer today takes approximately 20 seconds of browsing the web and one click of the mouse. When you attend a career fair and visit every table, of course you are not accomplishing anything you couldn't have done from your own computer in the privacy of your own home. Remember, at the next career fair you attend, choose 5 or 6 employers to speak with where you can leave a positive impact with, learn a little more about the firm by asking good questions, and give the employer the opportunity to learn something valuable about you. This type of effective networking cannot be done on the internet.

Another complaint which is also expressed by students in fields other than finance and accounting is, "Why aren't there any employers who are from a company in my field?" This answer is rather simple. There are plenty of accounting, auditing and financial firms in existence so accounting and finance majors as a rule tend not to have difficultly finding firms which provide open positions at their firm in their field of study. Marketing and human resources majors on the contrary often approach me stating that they could not find any marketing or human resources companies who were recruiting. What is the problem here? There is no problem here actually is the correct answer. Why are there not many marketing and human resource firms at career fairs opposed to accounting and financial firms? It is simply because there are not many, if any pure marketing or human resources companies in existence. The job of the student however is that he/she must approach an accounting or financial firm of their choice at a career fair and inquire about open positions in each of these firms' marketing or human resource departments. It is true that there are many accounting and financial firms compared to marketing and human resources firms, however every accounting and financial firm must have a marketing or human resources department in order to be successful. There are plenty of open positions that exist out there in corporate America, but no firm is going to advertise for you to apply to them individually. As you will read later in this book, you will learn that finding a job is not always about obtaining the one that everyone knows about or the employer that has interviewed half of the students in your business school. Networking and job searching is often about taking the back door to find a position which is most suitable for you at a firm. I myself have done this more often in my career than the traditional method and have been successful at becoming employed with some of the largest firms in America. This was one of my motivations in writing this book. I wanted to share my experiences with many students all across America so that they can become successful and attain their dreams and goals. Most students who are motivated, but have difficulty attaining jobs are much smarter than they give themselves credit. They just become hard on themselves because they do not fully understand what employers are actually looking for and expect from them. This is where this book can help.

Posture and eye contact is important when meeting with an employer. It is a good habit to always look someone in the eyes when you are speaking with them. Avoid looking over their shoulders or down at the ground. By looking someone in the eye it always indicates honesty, sincerity and confidence. The world of finance and sales looks for confident people to work for them. Why would a firm hire you as their representative to sell stocks and annuities to their clients if you are not confident in the products the company you are applying for is selling? Also good posture is important to an employer observing you. You should stand or sit up straight when someone is speaking to you. Lounging or leaning back shows disinterest to the employer to whom you are speaking. Talking with your hands as you speak is a good way to make the employer comfortable with you during a conversation. Be careful you do not use hand movements which become distracting to your conversation or place your hands in your pockets, however small movements are good to use and eliminate any nervousness you are feeling.

Name and faces are always good to remember. If you can do this, you have already eliminated the biggest challenge, which is mastering the art of networking. Although it may be tough to remember a name, it definitely becomes only to your benefit if you can remember it. An employer will take notice that you have good listening skills and a great memory. The employer will also realize that you had a great interest in the information he/she conveyed to you in your past conversation.

As I had mentioned, remembering names may not always be easy so if you cannot remember a contact's name it is good to take note and remember a key fact or point from your conversation. For example, if you forgot that recruiter's name you really admired from Merrill Lynch but you remember all about a funds discussion you had at last year's career fair, re-introduce yourself and bring up the discussion you had from last year to refresh the recruiter's memory. It is alright to forget a name but show sincerity and apologize, then re-introduce yourself to the recruiter or employer. As long as you are being honest the recruiter will almost always not mind that you forgot his/her name. If they are meeting with hundreds or even thousands of students throughout the country each year, chances are that they forgot your name as well over a few months time.

Honesty and acknowledgement is the most important part when re-introducing yourself. You would just re-introduce yourself and say something along the lines of "Hello, my name is Mike Bottaro. I believe we met at last year's career fair. I was very interested in the programs Merrill Lynch has to offer its employees and what opportunities lie within the company which you were able to explain to me extremely clearly last year. Your explanation of your funds that you offer also helped me gain a greater understanding of the products your firm offers its clients. I also remember discussing how we share an interest in baseball and that you played for your company's softball team for after-work leisure. However I do apologize I have forgotten your name. What is your name again?" Here you have just expressed that you remember your conversation with the employer from over a year ago, you remember what he informed you that his firm has to offer stating specific topics, and one personalize comment to ensure that the two of you indeed had a personalized previous conversation.

Also when you do greet an employer, make sure you shake his/her hand. Make sure you give the employer a firm grip so he can gain a sense of confidence from you, however do not try to strangle the recruiter's hand either. A hand shake is simply a form of welcome greeting and shows respect. It is important that you open and close your conversation with employers, recruiters and co-workers with these types of postures.

A word of advice is if you do not know an employer's name, do not lie and pretend that you do. It could just end up in a disaster. For example, there are some tricks that you may use to figure out an employer's name without directly asking them what their name is and assuming they are not wearing a name tag. I had a friend in college who used to ask an employer how they spelled their last name. This always worked well for him until he used this technique and approached an employer whose name was Jim Fox. My friend asked him how he spelled his last name. The employer replied F.O.X. My friend really felt dumb from this point on and elected not to use this method. As I stated to you previously, along with the professional topics we will cover in this book, I also promise to have some fun with you and share some humorous stories which I have encountered over the years.

Another good habit to get into is always asking for a representative's business card after having a conversation with him/her. It is good to keep excellent contacts with people you have met throughout the business world. Business cards are a great way to keep all of your contacts handy. I would recommend after collecting enough business cards to purchase a rolodex so that you can neatly organize all of your contacts. A rolodex is a great item to be able to readily access and keep handy on your desktop. By keeping good records of your contacts you are also enhancing your organizational skills which employers look for in a candidate.

We have now discussed quite a bit about career fairs, however we still need to cover the importance of networking at recruitment business dinners and formal company dinners. These evenings are intended as an informal way for an employer to get to know you, however remember that you are still attending a company event. Just because you are not working at the moment or being evaluated on your job performance, does not mean that you are not being evaluated or looked at in other areas. This is a test for an employer to see what type of personality you possess outside the workforce. In a situation where you are attending a recruitment dinner they are observing your personality to see if you match the fit they are looking for at their firm.

Always remember even the most generous and kind employers are not giving you a free meal on them for no apparent reason. A recruiting dinner is what it sounds like. Well it may not be called this but when you meet with an employer in a large crowd of other applicants who are all attending for a common goal of being hired, this is the reason you can expect for receiving an invite. Employers will pay, at their expense, to find out what an applicant is like outside of the office. This is a good test for an employer and can actually be seen by them as a very long term cost efficient way of determining who the proper applicants are that they should hire.

Some of these points may seem like common sense, however often many applicants do not take the hint or ever fully understand what is the proper behavior for a formal business dinner evening. One thing that you should completely avoid is ordering excessive amounts of alcohol. It sounds like common sense, but as a co-op I have actually sat with and observed the other co-ops getting drunk in front of their managers after work. Not only does this show irresponsibility and immaturity, but you are also hiking up the price for your employer at their expense. Believe me your manager will not be impressed. I can tell you that my managers in the past were not impressed. Remember, there is a time and place for everything. No one ever said that you cannot go out with your friends to party and drink more than two drinks. However, you must realize there is a time and place for everything. A business social is not the time for a relaxed binging event.

Typically, I would recommend not ordering any type of alcoholic beverage at all. However if the situation is appropriate, for example a happy hour, one or two drinks may be acceptable. Again, here is where you have to scope out your co-workers and bosses. If no one else is ordering alcohol at your table I would refrain from ordering one at all. Always use the most conservative approach to situations like these and you will make the correct decision every time.

As for ordering food, when an employer invites you to attend a business dinner do not feel obligated that you must order only the cheapest appetizer on the menu for your main course at dinner, however it would be unnecessary to order a main lobster as well. Again use your best judgment in situations like these. When eating always remember to place the napkin on your lap and use your silverware, working from the outside to the inside. Your plates and soup bowls should never leave the table. This would indicate poor table manners. While cutting your food, never cut all your food at once. This could make you appear like a child who needs all his food cut for him before he eats his food. This may sound silly but depending on how picky an employer is, he/she might take notice to these behaviors. The safe bet is to cut approximately three to five pieces of your entree before each time you eat.

Finally, when a toast is made, regardless whether you choose to drink the champagne or not you should not draw any unnecessary attention to yourself. If you wish to drink the champagne during a toast, you may go ahead and do so. If you do not wish to drink the champagne, that is perfectly fine as well, however you should still raise your glass when the room cheers and then place your glass back exactly where you picked it up from on the table. If you do not want to drink it that is fine, as long as you don't announce it to your entire table, turn your glass upside down, or something else which would draw unnecessary attention to yourself. If you announce to a room that you can't drink the champagne or alcoholic drink which is being toasted, it can often indicate to others that you could possibly be a recovered alcoholic. Even thought this is most likely not true, you never even want to put such thoughts in the minds of your employers and co-workers.

Now that we have discussed the proper etiquette for networking with an employer and trying to set up an interview, I think we are ready to move to Chapter 5 where we will discuss tips for interviewing. Chapter 5 will probably be the most detailed chapter in this book. It will be crucial that you take notes so that you can be prepared for your next interview. By following these networking tips discussed in this chapter, you should be well prepared to enter your interview. You have already impressed the employer enough to obtain an interview. Now the employer will want to find out what you have to offer their firm. It is important that you be well prepared to answer their questions that they will have for you. Often there are questions that become repetitive by nearly all interviewers. My goal in the next chapter is to inform you of what these questions are and how to prepare you well for them when an interviewer asks you these types of questions.

CHAPTER 5

Interviewing Skills

One of the most stressful times in the majority of Americans is the time when they enter an interview. Interviewing may indeed seem like one of the most stressful hour or two of your life, but in reality it should not be. Think of it this way, stay calm and the worst they can say is that you didn't get the job. I can assure you that regardless what type of rejection you are feeling, you should not be too hard on yourself. There are plenty of other opportunities that lie ahead which are probably even a better fit for you than the job you applied to and didn't get. The definition of an interview can be described as:

in·ter·view [in-ter-vyoo]—*noun*
a formal meeting in which one or more persons question, consult, or evaluate another person: *a job interview.*

Can you decipher which are the key words in this definition? If your response is the words formal and evaluate you are correct! You could argue that question and consult may be two of the most important words, however you know previous to entering an interview that they are going to ask you a series of questions about yourself. What I need to stress is actually how you can answer them when they are evaluating you in a formal matter. Notice I included both of those words (formal and evaluating) in my response.

In this chapter I will cover more information than any other chapter in the book. There is by far the most to discuss about interviewing because it is the most heavily weighted part in an employer's job decision process as to whether or not they want to hire you. When I originally decided to begin writing this book, this chapter was the first impression I had for what I wanted my book's content to include. As I began brainstorming, I quickly realized that there were several other important aspects of the job hiring process by employers which would be crucial to include in this book for an applicant like yourself to be confident and successful when approaching any situation he/she may face throughout their career.

Interviews may be stressful for most people, but after you read this chapter, my goal for each and everyone of you is to realize that the interview process shouldn't be stressful and for you to become confident and stress-free before entering your next interview.

One of the most important things to remember when interviewing is that you are a salesman. It would be a fair assessment to state that interviewing is very similar to sales. The art of interviewing is the ability to sell or market yourself. If you aren't confident in what you are selling or what you have to offer, how is the employer interviewing you going to be confident about hiring you? Work experience and interviewing practice will make you become a perfectionist when selling yourself to others. Honesty and integrity are one's most valuable assets. These traits are what make up any successful salesman's reputation and are dependent upon his future progression of remaining successful. The same traits are crucial when interviewing as well. Your reputation will be backed by describing to an employer your past accomplishments and the professional references you provide. Sales should always be looked at as a hobby. You should be passionate about what you are selling and enjoy doing it. If you are interviewing and can enjoy having a conversation with an employer about your work experience and future goals you will master the art of interviewing. It is important to sell yourself to an employer in a manner that would make them want to buy (hire) you. Remember, an interview is your time to shine. In reality an interview is all about you. Highlight your work and education history. Talk most heavily about accomplishments, achievements and things you have done of which you are proud.

On the contrary, it is indeed probably true that you have worked for a place which you did not enjoy or had a bad experience with, however you want to refrain from making an employer aware of this. You can use one example from this if an employer asks in an interview to describe a difficult situation where you had to make an impact to change things or make significant areas of improvement to resolve the problem. I have had this question asked to me in numerous interviews. This can be a difficult question, however remember to save the negative job experience for this question. When you do describe the situation to the employer, also make sure that you always bring a positive out-come from the problem you were faced with. An employer here is not asking what problems have you had in the past. You must read between the lines in an interview. Reading between the lines to fully understand what an employer is really asking you or wants to learn about you is one of the most important skills to develop in order to seal a good interview. What an employer is really asking here is how can you overcome an adverse situation.

Nearly everyone has had a bad work experience. It would be a lie if you said that you had never been faced with a difficult situation in your life time, how-ever, the bottom line is that the positives should always heavily outweigh the negatives when discussing your previous job experiences with an employer. You want to position that the reason you are applying for this new job at their firm is to better your career and not to get away from that last lousy job that you held. As you read further into this book, you will learn the art and tech-nique to positioning. What your response is to an employer is not always what he/she is taking biggest note to, but it is how you position your response.

Previously I had worked for one of the largest mutual fund providers world wide. I worked in their retail services department selling mutual funds and IRAs. The company had sent out a survey to all of their clients asking them which were the most important factors to them when they spoke with a repre-sentative at our firm. The choice included words (employees used) and their tone of voice. The results reflected that an overwhelming 86% of our custom-ers were more affected with how our employees were able to relate to our cus-tomers and their tone of voice, opposed to the 14% who said the employees' choice of words and content were most important to their customer service relationship. The content which you are conveying in response to an employer's question is certainly important, however you also want to make sure that your tone of voice and confidence level is high so that an employer will respect your personality and feel comfortable communicating and work-ing with you in the future.

The interview time is now here. You have a solid understanding of what personality you need to possess going into the interview. Recapping from Chapter 3, you know what is the only suitable form of attire to wear to your interview, which is business formal of course. Now it is time for you to be aware of what questions an interviewer may ask you and how to be well pre-pared to answer these types of questions.

The phone rings, the secretary from Morgan Stanley's office in West Ches-ter, NY calls. Morgan Stanley has been your dream firm throughout four years of college and now you finally have the wonderful opportunity to interview with the company. The secretary confirms a time and place with you and informs you that she will send you a confirmation e-mail to inform you whom you will be meeting with and directions to their facility. Remember, when you are given the name of whom you are expected to meet with, make a note of the person's name so that you are ready to greet them when you meet them for the first time on your interview day. This shows respect and your interest to the interviewer. You then thank the secretary for setting up the appointment and hang up the phone. A few days have passed, and the day now has finally arrived when you will be meeting with Morgan Stanley for a first interview. You then should button up your white dress shirt, wear your crimson red tie, button up your navy blue suit and be on your way.

When you have an interview scheduled, always remember to give yourself plenty of time to reach your destination. For example, if you know that the company's facility is located an hour away, it wouldn't be a bad idea to give yourself two hours in case you run into traffic or cannot find the building. This is especially an important habit to get into if you are not familiar with the area in which your interview's facility is located. There is nothing worse than arriving late to a first interview. This already shows irresponsibility and poor time management skills. Ideally you should arrive for any first interview approximately 10-15 minutes early. This gives you plenty of time to check in with the receptionist, relax, use the bathroom or grab a glass of water before you begin to meet with your interviewer. You can never arrive for an interview too early. If you arrive much earlier than scheduled, you can always sit in the building's lobby or your car and gather your last thoughts together before your interview.

It is now 1:45pm and your interview is scheduled for 2:00pm. You walk to the receptionist and politely state your name, thank her, and take a seat. 2:00pm sharp is now here and you see an unfamiliar face call your name. You should immediately shake the person's hand and greet him/her with something along the lines of "It is a pleasure to meet you." The interview has now officially begun. Note: Always make sure that you make excellent eye contact with the interviewer while maintaining a firm handshake.

Both you and the employers take your seats and an employer may first ask you if you have an extra copy of your resume. I would always advise having at least three copies of your resume handy upon entering an interview. Also it is important to have a ball point pen with you, a list of questions that you have prepared to ask the employer towards the end of the interview when he/she opens the discussion for questioning and extra scrap paper to take notes.

Always ask an employer if he is comfortable with you taking notes. In almost all cases he/she will not only be fine with you taking notes, but will actually encourage it so that you can maximize the efficiency and learning process of the interview. This shows your expressed interest in their firm. Being able to jot notes down throughout the interview helps you regroup your thoughts. Be careful, although it is great to take notes it is still important to keep good eye contact. I would advise writing a word or two here and there, not full sentences.

You now should be prepared for your first question. You never can know what to expect first. Every interviewer has a completely different style of interviewing. This is why I must prepare you well for all scenarios. You will often find some interviews are very laid back and you leave feeling great about the person with whom you met. Other times you will interview with one of the toughest people you have ever met who will try to stump you by throwing all types of outrageous questions at you. The important thing to remember here is to stay calm and focused.

As I mentioned, you can't possibly know what the first question that will be asked by an employer, however what you can do is practice a few of the most typical first questions an employer commonly asks a candidate. I stress these first questions so much because the first question sets the tone for the interview. If you do not give an answer remotely to what an employer is looking for, in reality the interview is over within the first 30 seconds. This will also create awkward tension for the remainder of the interview. If you can give a great response to the first question however, it will set a wonderful tone for the rest of the interview process and you will be amazed how much stress has been eliminated allowing you to calm down and easily answer the following questions.

"Tell me about yourself." This is often the first question out of an employer's mouth. This is probably the most basic question an employer can ask you and yet it often becomes the most difficult for a candidate to answer. How you should appropriately answer the question would be to state briefly your previous few employers, your work and education experiences including where you graduated from and why you are interested in this firm to which you are applying. You would then follow these statements by linking your previous experiences to the firm which you are interviewing with by expressing how you can effectively make a contribution to their firm. You should be able to include all of this information in no more than 30-40 seconds. Please try not to be too wordy. Just like your resume, you want to be concise and to the point. This is not the question to beat around the bush and discuss your family life and your hobbies. It may sound cruel, but at this stage of your relationship with the person interviewing you, he/she does not care about what leisure activities or hobbies you have. This is true at least at this stage of the interview.

Remember, you have made it this far. You certainly have many skills and qualifications that make you marketable and worthy of obtaining the position. Make sure you bring these qualities to an employer's attention first and foremost. As I said before, an interview is all about you. It is your time to shine. Make the best of it.

Another first question an employer may ask you is, "Why are you here?" or "What made you decide to apply and want to work here?" You should always be well prepared for these types of questions. This is why you should have your research complete on the company with which you are interviewing. This question will then become easy for you to answer. Again you want to state a few facts about the company which you feel are important, your ethical beliefs, and the values of what the company expressed. You then should relate your past job experiences quickly to the subject matter explaining why you are a qualified candidate and match for the company that is interviewing you. You must remember, a company's first impression and objective with its applicants is not how they can hire you, but how they can eliminate you. Often an employer is interviewing hundreds or even thousands of college students each year. The process' beginning step in first interviews is to reduce the number of candidates so that they can narrow their choices in a second interview and focus on their top considerations. It is important that you have an understanding of how to answer these questions so that you can make the cut. You can relate the interviewing process to when you are trying to make a competitive high school level or college sports team. The first day several athletes are cut and released. You need to practice just like athletes so that your performance is top of your game and so that you can outperform the competition.

The first 30-40 seconds of your interview is crucial to grab the employer's attention. I like to call this short-time period your "30 second elevator speech." For instance, say that you were on an elevator which you walked on from the lobby. You are headed to the 34th floor of the building. When the elevator stops on the 4th floor, the doors open and the C.E.O. of the company you have always wanted to work for is standing beside you. You have thirty seconds. Think fast! What do you say to him? The same rule applies to the first few seconds of the interview you are on. You must remain professional and have a quick line or two prepared which you would want to ask him/her in a situation like this. The same 30 second rule applies to an interview.

The first 30-40 seconds are possibly more important than the next 30-40 minutes. You can compare this to a public speech in front of an audience, a commercial, or even a stand-up comedian. If you loose the audience's attention in the first few seconds, you have lost their attention for the entire speech or presentation. This is a fact of life. Your audience is the employer or employers interviewing you just as the crowd and television viewers are for a stand-up comedian on stage. In this situation, however you are not telling any crude jokes. You should have an easier task as well, you only have one or two observers at the moment. The stand-up comedian has millions of viewers watching him.

So you made it! You nailed the first question. Congratulations! The interviewer is still awake and interested in what you are answering. If you have made it this far while still keeping the interest of the employer you have already covered a general discussion of your previous employment history, educational background and why you can become a valuable asset and contributor to the firm if hired for the position.

Next, you can expect a variety of different questions which an employer may ask you. From my experiences, here is a list of the most commonly asked questions when interviewing with an employer.

- What do you know about our company?

- What are your strengths?

- What are your weaknesses?

- Demonstrate how you best have been a leader.

- How would your boss or last employer describe you?

- What are your expectations of our company?

- What are your future goals?

- What attributes would your ideal job include?

- Name one or two of the most important decisions that you have made in your life.

- What important trends do you see in our industry?

- Describe a time when you took the initiative to complete a project which may have seemed difficult to accomplish at school or work.

- What is the biggest risk you ever took?

- What were some of your favorite college classes?

- What were some of your least favorite college classes?

- Describe a time where you worked as a team to complete a task.

- What experience do you have in this field of business?

- Describe some of the recent market trends in comparison to the performance of our company in recent history.

- List a time where you went above and beyond to complete a task that was not required of you.

- Why should we hire you?

Expect these questions to be frequently asked by an employer in an interview. There are always going to be job specific questions which may arise, however if you can practice having a response for all of these questions you will at least be able to answer the majority of the employer's questions effectively. Make sure you are prepared before going into an interview. If you can answer all of the previous questions, then you will have a solid discussion in your next interview. "Practice makes perfect." With each interview, you will find these questions much easier to answer. Not only because you have read this book and practiced these types of questions, but that you have gained more work experience and you should have many more examples which you can discuss when answering an interviewer's question.

Remember, whenever answering any of the above questions which an interviewer may ask you, always remain calm and be prepared to answer each question with a response and a specific example of how you demonstrated those skills or carried out those functions. For example, you may be asked the question "Demonstrate how you have best been a leader." (Companies love to see ambition and leadership qualities in their candidates.) Explain why you are a leader by stating, "I am a leader because I have taken initiative to put in no less than 110% effort and have succeeded throughout my career while setting an example for my peers, co-workers and classmates throughout college." That is an excellent start. Now, here comes the tricky part. You have only completed half of your response. You have to prove or convince this potential employer you have possessed this skill. This is the point where you need to give specific examples of times you have demonstrated leadership skills. When using examples to prove a point I think listing your examples is always a good approach. By listing your points, I mean when an employer asks you to give an example of a specific time you have demonstrated yourself as a leader, it is good to respond with an answer such as, "I can give you three examples." Then you would begin to list your three examples. By giving an employer a list, it allows you to organize the interviewer's thoughts. When you give a list it also paints an organized picture for the employer. These types of lists grasp the attention of the employer to the key points which you are trying to make. Also, some people are visual learners while others are verbal learners. When you give a list for an employer, you are not only speaking to the employer verbally, but you are also painting a picture in the employer's head.

It is true this technique may not always help you obtain the job during the interview process, but it can't hurt you either. Think of it in a mathematical sense. By conveying your examples of success to an employer in a broader sense, it will significantly increase your chances of getting the job because you are relating to an audience twice the size of your original strategy. It is always important to take all strategies into consideration. You never know which situation will win you the job.

Here is a great example of how to answer the question, "Demonstrate how you best have been a leader." It can be answered, using only your similar experiences. You will answer, "I can give you three ways. First, I have taken initiative to join a professional organization at school and strived to be a leader until I obtained the position as Executive Vice President. There I was able to assist in developing not only my own career ambitions, but the professional progression of my classmates. Second, I had taken the initiative to obtain value experience throughout my internships during my summer vacation time off. There I was able to experience the world of corporate finance in a hands-on atmosphere. Third and finally, I have grown up in family possessing strong work ethics and careful decision making. I have taken these ethics into account and have strived to make others around me better as well. Throughout the Financial Management Association I have learned that it is important to pick good people as your successors. Good people make a good company or organization. The people who you choose as executive team members or board members are the ones who will best carry on the work you have created. You often want members with experience to take on these roles. Often there are a limited number of positions which can be filled by several excellent candidates. In these situations, it is important to acknowledge hard work from those with less seniority and enhance their knowledge so that one day they can possibly fit into this type of roll. Even if their time is not now, if they are dedicated people who have the motivation to learn, they may one day be ready to fulfill the role. These are my three examples of leadership based on what I have learned in my past experiences."

What most people don't realize is interviewing is often just relating or sharing common ideas with another person. Nearly every interview I have ever went on, I knew in the first 30 seconds of the interview if I was going to obtain the position or not. At least 95% of the time, my instincts were correct.

Interviews are two sided however. When I say "two sided" I mean you are interviewing the employer as well. If something doesn't feel right about the position, you weren't impressed because of their lack of professionalism, or you didn't enjoy speaking with the person interviewing you, it is usually an accurate indication that it is not the right place for you to work. Even if they offer you a position, if you weren't comfortable interviewing with them, it probably wouldn't be a good idea to accept the position. It is important to value your profession as a proud career or hobby and not a job. When you accept a position you are not thrilled with, ultimately you will not be happy. This theory is true, even if the job you find boring pays much more than the other job which best fits your dream career path.

It is important to know what you want in your career and apply to only positions where you feel you will be most happy. You want to make sure that your goals match the goals of the employer interviewing you. It is always good to be ambitious and prove it to an employer. It is wonderful to have goals, however if you have too many career goals aside from the position you are applying for an employer may feel the position is not your top priority. Ultimately, this could reflect the employer's decision of hiring you because he/she may feel you have too many distractions in your personal business life. My message to my readers is not to lack personal ambitions, however be cautious as to how many of your goals you discuss with an employer. When an employer hires you, he/she is viewing you as a long-term investment and if they feel you are not putting their company first, they may feel you are not the best candidate. I admire and applaud you if you are the type of motivated person who can handle two jobs, however be careful and use your best judgment on how much detail you wish to convey to an employer. Each situation is unique when discussing personal career goals. If you are ever uncertain how much to share with an employer, stop and think what you would want to hear from a candidate if you were interviewing them for a position at your company. If you make your major points clear to an employer in an interview that your goals are to grow with their company, they will be enthused with your response and you will instantly make yourself more marketable for them hiring you.

While interviewing, if there is ever something the employer is discussing which you do not understand, ask him to pause and ask for clarity. This is good because this is mastering the art of "checking." Once employed or hired by a firm, an employer will assume that you will be doing this so that you can effectively gather all the correct answers necessary to do your job. By asking these types of questions in an interview it is a good start.

It is important, however, that you remain polite and do not interrupt the employer either. Use you best judgment as to when are the most appropriate times to ask an employer questions. Just as a rule of thumb, always let an employer do as much talking as possible. If he is not questioning you at the moment, sit tight and hold your questions or comments for after he has completed his thought.

You know when an interview is nearing to a close when the employer asks if you have any questions for him/her. Even though this is one of the final steps of the process, it could be the longest if you have prepared a long list of questions for them. Always make sure you have a minimum of three or four questions for them. Even if an employer comes forward and indicates to you it is not necessary for any further questions I would still ask him if he didn't mind answering the few questions that you did have prepared for him. It is important to let an employer know that you are interested in learning more about the position at the company which you are applying for. Other times, an employer may only have three or four questions for you and he/she then leaves the floor open to you for questioning them for the next hour. This incident has happened to me before as well and that is why I would recommend having ten or twelve questions prepared for an employer just in case this situation was to occur. The employer said to me after five minutes of interviewing me, "Ok sir, now it's your turn to interview me." This actually was one of the most difficult interviews I have ever been on.

When discussing first round interviews, what are good questions to ask an employer? The answer is it really depends. Depending on what field or type of job you are applying for, it will change what types of questions you should be asking an employer. Remember to have well thought questions created before interviewing with an employer. Part of your evaluation by an employer will be the types of questions you challenge him/her with as well. As long as you have prepared a few good questions with at least one being company specific you will be fine during this stage of the interview. Remember to have your pen handy and take notes during this part so that you can show your strong interest to the employer's response. It can also help you to glance at your paper so you are ready to fire the next question at them after receiving an answer to your last question. The worst thing that can happen during this stage of an interview is to be completely stumped or when they ask you if you have any questions at all, and you reply, "No. I really have no questions about your firm." That would be a strong indication of lack of preparation. It is possible that if the employer has answered most of your questions throughout the interview, that is why it is so important to have 10 or 12 questions prepared so that you have a wider variety of questions to ask him. In some cases you may only need to ask 2 or 3 questions. Regardless, asking 2 or 3 questions is always better than none.

Make sure you always ask for the employer's permission before taking notes, however most will not mind. Actually most of the employers who have interviewed me over the years have seemed quite impressed or flattered that I would want to write down their feedback. Just be careful not to read directly from your questions. Only use your sheet of prepared questions as an outline to organize your thoughts. Taking notes is always a good habit. Often this will indicate to an employer that you are also a good note taker and are well organized. It may be an indication to him/her that you document all of your work and findings. Documentation is crucial in any position in the business world and in almost all other professions. What you learn from your experiences can be documented as proof or for the learning process of other employees whom are employed at your firm in future situations. Learning from your peers is one of the most effective ways to learn from mistakes and previous experiences. My last boss always used a phrase and I never forgot it. He said, "In God we trust. Everyone else puts it in writing." I always thought that expression was shown to be humorous, however very true.

When asking the employer questions towards the end of an interview it is always good to be well prepared. It is now your turn to interview the employer.

You must be well prepared because just as an employer would be unimpressed if you couldn't answer any of his questions, wouldn't you be unimpressed if you entered an interview and the employer stares as to say to you, "I forget what I was going to ask you today." It sounds silly but now you can see the importance of being prepared to answer an employer's questions and ask the right questions of them as well.

What questions are good to ask an employer? Below I will list categories of general questions which are typically good to ask an employer followed by some more job specific questions. Here is the list of questions I think would be most relevant to ask an employer.

- What is a typical work day like?

- What qualities or attributes would make someone successful in this position?

- Communications, internal and external, are clearly important to your firm. What are the related priorities for this role?

- What is a typical career path I can expect?

- What departments will I be working with?

- What is the most rewarding aspect of your job?

- What is it about this company that would make me want to work here?

- What are some challenges I may face?

- If someone were to come into this role and make a significant impact on culture and morale, what type of changes would you, management, the board, and the C.E.O. want to see most? How would this be measured?

- What types of software are used?

- Based on this discussion, is there anything you feel would prevent me from doing well in this position?

These are all fair game general questions which you may ask an employer when you are called to ask him/her questions. Next, if you are in a specific field of finance such as financial advising, these are the types of questions that may help you as well.

Questions for a Financial Advisor

- What are typical clients like and how have their portfolios performed?

- How many clients do you have? What is their average portfolio size?

- What is the client/broker ratio?

- How important is it to have a well-written financial plan or Investment Policy Statement (IPS)?

- What licensing is required for this position?

On a first interview, the only types of questions you should definitely avoid asking are salary questions. If the employer comes forward about discussing these numbers first then it is certainly appropriate to discuss this information with him/her. The rule here is that you never want to be the one who initiates this conversation. The same theory holds true for asking about benefits and vacation time. These are definitely important considerations when choosing a job, however you do not want to be over anxious about asking these types of questions either. If you ask an employer how much vacation time you get as your first question, the employer may respond, "How about a permanent vacation. Your time begins today!" Relax, the employer will eventually come forward and discuss salary, benefits and vacation with you. In the meantime, remain patient and this will eventually be discussed. In a second interview this may be appropriate to inquire about if a second interview were to take place and the employer had not mentioned salary information throughout the entire first interview. We will discuss these points next when we begin to discuss interviews which have a second and third follow-up interview.

Professionalism is one of the most important skills to maintain throughout an interview process. Without remaining professional, rarely you will be able to impress an employer and obtain a decent job. However at times, an employer may not always remain professional either. Is this appropriate? Certainly not, but do not fall into his/her trap and act in an unprofessional manner either. You may be falling into their trap of observing how you will react to their actions. I can tell you that you will rarely encounter this type of behavior, but it is possible. For example, I have a friend who was once asked on an interview, "Do you love your wife and kids?" This is a rather inappropriate and irrelevant question. I have also come across people who were asked, "How is your sex life?" These may seem extreme and bizarre, but they do occur in rare situations. Remember to remain polite, but refuse to answer these types of questions in all situations. The employer may be testing to see how smart you are, if you can stand up for yourself, or even how you react to a stressful and difficult situation in the workforce.

Now that we have completely covered first round interviews, we can begin to discuss second and third round interviews. Second and third round interviews will be rather shortly discussed in length compared to first round interviews due to the overlap which will occur between the interviews. Often second and third interviews exist solely so that after interviewing numerous candidates in a first round interview, they can then spend more time to get to know their candidates in a second or third round interview. Often second and third round interviews may include the opportunity to be shown a tour of their facility, take a personality test, work as a team in groups with other applicants, and/or have more informal conversations with each other establishing a post-hire relationship.

When closing an interview you should always thank the employer for taking the time to meet with you before your departure. It would be a good idea to ask the employer for his business card so that you can remain in contact with him/her and then shake their hand. Finally, ask the employer when they will be making their decision and ask about an approximate time frame of when you can expect to hear from them about a possible job opportunity. It is good to be polite and keep good contacts because just because you do not get hired right on the spot or within a few weeks with a company, doesn't mean they did not want to hire you. Unfortunately sometimes there are only a limited amount of open positions. It would not be out of the question if an employer were to call you back at a later date and extend an offer a few months later. This is why keeping good contacts can be helpful in the long run.

A thank you note is always appropriate to send every employer after interviewing with them. It would be a good idea to create a business letter and send it by U.S. mail on the day of the interview immediately after the interview. An employer usually makes his decision within a few business days, so it would be a good idea to send the letter so that it will be received by the employer before he/she makes his decision. A typical thank you note does not need to be long in length. You are simply thanking the employer for his/her time to meet with you and stating that you hope to speak with them soon. You could also add in an extra sentence or two if you wish, describing something in your interview which you were impressed by and made you want to work for their firm even more. Thank you notes are always a good idea. I would recommend this to be mandatory if you are seriously considering obtaining the job. Even if the employer does not judge its candidates on if they received a thank you note or not, in a difficult decision between two candidates and you sent a thank you and they did not, this could be the difference in you obtaining the job and the other candidate not getting the job. Thank you notes express politeness and strong interest.

Another helpful tip for interviewing is to make sure you look at interviews as practice. Do not be discouraged if you are not hired by the first one or two employers you interview with. The more interviews you go on, the more you will become comfortable with how to interview with employers in all situations. With every interview you go on you will become closer to mastering the art of a perfect interview. Always save the companies whom which you are most interested in for interviewing last. This is a good idea so that you have had a great deal of practice interviewing with the previous companies before your final interview, which is your most important. By this point you have already gathered a good idea of what the other firms in the industry may ask you during their interview process.

As we move on to Chapter 6 we will begin to learn more about how to handle an interview with a case study. These case studies are usually team oriented and observed by employers so that they can observe how you work with others to resolve a problem or create a solution. These typically occur in second and third round interviews as well. Now that you have a solid understanding of what an interviewer is looking for in a candidate during the interview process, you will find yourself becoming well prepared to work on a case study with other candidates. You will find that the 4 Major Skills from Chapter 1 will play a huge factor in impressing your employer.

CHAPTER 6

Case Study Skills

Case Studies are one of the more modern ways which employers evaluate their applicants today. Case studies usually occur in a second or third interview, typically by a large size corporation, who has a new hire or rotational program. Companies feel that before they make the long-term investment of hiring a new candidate for employment, they want to be sure that they have selected a candidate who has proven that they can work in groups with co-workers to complete a common goal. Participation and cooperation are mandatory if you wish to be hired by the firm.

Typically in an interview process, if you made it this far, you most likely got the job. However, it still is not over. You can never be certain that you have the job. Also, you still want to make the best use of the time you have with the employer to impress them and show that you can communicate well with others while working in a leader role as a team with your possible future co-workers. Often in these case studies you will have only a limited amount of time to collaborate as a group and come up with an answer. If you have ever watched the television show "The Apprentice" hosted by Donald Trump, the projects they assign on that show can be closely correlated with the concept of these case studies.

Typically an employer will not give you enough time to gather the correct answer with 100% accuracy, however the assignment is observed more around your theory and thought process. Often the employer will not even provide you with all the proper resources needed to solve the problem. This is quite alright because the employer already knows this is a problem. The case is meant to be a challenge. What you will have to do is explain why you arrived at the conclusion which you chose.

After the employer assigns you a team and hands you a case, you will then need to start to collaborate ideas and begin to resolve the problem. The answer is rarely obvious, actually it is never obvious. You will then need to brainstorm and consider all the possible alternatives with your team for a solution. For each solution you will also need to state how you derived the answer you chose by explaining your thought process and steps to achieve the goal.

Communication skills will be observed by your employer as you are constantly discussing different alternatives in your group. In order to be a good communicator, one needs to be a good listener as well. A good communicator will not only provide the groups with their ideas, but listen to the ideas of others and provide them with feedback. Communication is the backbone to any corporation's operations. This is why an employer assigns these types of activities.

Teamwork skills will be noticed as well while working with your group members. An employer will be taking notes of how well you accept the ideas of others. The efficiency of how well your group works together will also be measured. The goal of your team should be to gather all of your unique ideas together so that you can agree on a common conclusion to the case's problem. This may be the single most important skill to have in order to master a case study or presentation in the interviewing process.

In one case study experience of mine when interviewing with a financial firm, I was called to give a presentation describing how teamwork impacts work efficiency in a corporation. The presentation which I gave was to an audience of approximately 20 people who wanted me to give specific examples of how I have become a team player and how I could transition it to the corporate finance world. I opened up with a background history of myself and the definition of teamwork to break the ice. I then transitioned it to my previous internship experiences and my academic life as an executive officer of a professional organization. Make sure you open and close your speech strong. You must always grab your audience's attention and also leave them remembering the last lines you said. A quote somewhere in the middle of your speech is always a good idea as well. When I gave my presentation, I quoted the C.E.O. of Merrill Lynch indirectly speaking about the importance of teamwork. A few years ago when Merrill Lynch held a press conference for its clients and shareholders, an elderly woman spoke up and asked the C.E.O. of Merrill Lynch if he was aware that he employs numerous advisors who made more money than he did at the company last year. The C.E.O. replied, "Yes. I know. I wish all my advisors made more money than I did." This was an excellent answer. Financial advisors rely heavily on commissions and sales in the securities industry. The answer was clear to the public. He was most interested in the progress and long-term growth for Merrill Lynch by his staff working as a team. The amount of money his advisors make reflects the performance of this evaluation. When a C.E.O. or president's financial advisors perform well and make more money, it ultimately reflects his salary and reputation in the eyes of the public. I think this statement also shows when teamwork dominates greed, it outperforms the level of success you will have throughout your career than if you didn't hold these teamwork values. The quote was able to complete my speech and my interviewers understood what teamwork meant to a student just graduating college. Employers will definitely recognize research you have done and knowledge which you possess. If you can make a transition with these skills to teamwork you will really be able to set yourself apart from the rest and become one step closer towards obtaining the job you are interviewing for.

Finally, the most important skill to possess during a case study is leadership. It is important to take the initiative to be a leader in your group. Everyone in your group may indeed agree to participate, however it is often difficult to find someone who will take ownership and responsibility for completing the project. As a team leader, you are the spokesperson for your group and the person whom others will contact if in need of guidance. An employer will respect you for assuming this role because it is an indicator that you are not afraid to take on additional responsibility. It also indicates to an employer that you may have potential for a management position one day. It is good to set yourself from the other applicants by taking responsibility and volunteering for different roles in your young career.

Leadership is such an important quality to develop because employers take notice of employees' ability to go above and beyond what is required. This also translates to finding which candidates or employees would make excellent future managers. It is important to recognize what leadership is derived from. Leadership is developed through two major motivations. These motivations include "Toward Gain" and "Prevent Pain." Nearly everyone has one of these motivations, however, having only one of these motivations does not make up an excellent leader. It is important to possess a balance of both and always maintain a motivated attitude. Most employees do possess the motivation of preventing pain. "Prevent Pain" includes the motivation to complete the things you are required to do. These things may include the daily operations which you are called to complete in your daily list of tasks given to you by your manager. "Toward Gain" on the other hand is motivation which you are not required to possess. "Toward Gain" actions by an employee may include taking part in a project or problem case which you volunteer to help with, that is not included in your daily scope of work. In this case, you have exceeded your expectations and have probably caught the eye of your employer. Most employees lack the trait of toward gain because it is not a mandatory task assigned to them. It is your responsibility to exceed average performance and participation in the work place so that you can distinguish yourself from all other candidates and employees.

There are several different categories of cases which an employer may ask its candidates to resolve. So that you can become familiar with what types of questions may be asked, I will provide you with an example. This will allow you to better answer an employer's questions if you are ever called to resolve a case study as a group. Some sample questions of what an employer may ask its candidates include something similar to these examples.

Your room's candidates are broken into two separate teams. The only information you are given in advance is that you will be solving a problem case regarding the satellite radio industry. Then an index card is handed out to each group. Group 1 and Group 2 have different questions regarding the same industry. Then you are told you have 5 minutes to find an answer. The clock starts now.

Group1

Question:

Sirius and XM, the satellite radio networks, have consumed enormous amounts of capital while compiling a record of huge loses. Will these companies ever be profitable? What must they do to achieve profitability?

An Acceptable Answer:

Satellite radio is a relatively new industry which for investors has created high possible returns in exchange for taking high risks. At the current moment the company is expected to have low earnings due to the high costs of purchasing satellites. However there is long-term potential for the companies due to the quick growth rates of the companies in the industry. Company growth would indicate paying few dividends to its shareholders, and re-investing them back into the company's share price to raise more capital. As more users purchase satellite radio, the companies in the industry such as Sirius and XM will become successful. The bottom line with satellite radio companies having high fixed expenses is they should advertise and market as efficiently as possible while still keeping their budget low. Cutting costs and receiving more customers will be the keys to making the company profitable in the long run.

Group 2

Question:

Sirius and XM, the satellite radio networks, have losses yet their stocks have substantial market capitalization. How do you value companies like this?

An Acceptable Answer:

The substantial market capitalization shown is derived from a growth stock company such as Sirius or XM who re-invest a large portion of their dividends into their share price instead of distributing them to its shareholders. Companies are able to value this by calculating the value of future cash flows. Also calculating basic financial ratios are important in valuing a company such as Price/Share, Price/Book Value, Price/Cash Flow, and E.B.I.T.D.A. (All of these are financial ratios which are used by analysts who try to valuate a company or try to estimate an accurate price for what a company is worth before making a merge or acquisition.)

The bottom line to mastering a case study is to not worry if you do not answer every case study perfectly. I wanted to give you an example situation with answers so that you can use it as a guide to address the situation when you are faced with these cases. Remember, communicate efficiently, work as a team, take initiative to lead your team and remain open to all opinions of your teammates. You will find yourself being able to effectively help your team reach its goals by taking these most professional actions. Case studies are more common sense than other areas we have discussed in the interviewing process, however it is still important to realize what employers are observing and looking for when you are called to present. Case studies should not be stressful.

In the next chapter however, you will find it much more difficult to remain calm when you are faced with trick questions which an employer may expect from you. These questions will typically catch you off guard and an employer is looking for your reaction under pressure. Learning how to respond to trick questions is my favorite part of this book. I think you will enjoy learning how to respond to these types of questions as well. Once you get a feel for how to answer a few examples which I will provide, you will then be prepared to answer any challenging questions which you are faced with over your career. I promise we will have some fun discussing these types of questions in the next chapter.

CHAPTER 7

Trick Interview Questions

Trick interview questions are exactly what they sound like. An employer will often throw a question at you that may seem bizarre and is irrelevant to the job's role. So why do employers ask these questions? The answer is an employer wants to observe how its candidates react under pressure and their thought process under stressful situations which quickly arise in the corporate world. After reading this chapter, it will become obvious to you when you are being asked a trick question. Next time when you go into an interview and are asked a trick question, you may not answer the question correctly, however you will at least know how to react and how to begin attempting to solve it.

When you are asked these types of questions, the most important thing you must remember is that the employers themselves may not even know the correct answer. That's right! Often the person asking you the question does not know the answer to his own question. The interviewer may not even be fully listening once you give him your answer. The major thing he/she is taking note to is how you react and your posture. When asked these types of questions, you should identify that the employer has asked you a trick question, remain calm, and be prepared to start talking through your thought process out loud. Many times there is no correct answer to these types of questions.

There are many approaches you can take for giving an acceptable answer. The only incorrect answers you can give an employer are to say "I don't know" or completely freeze. If you react this way, the interview may not be over but it is going to be extremely difficult to win the interviewer back from this point forward. As long as you don't freak out, stay calm, and begin to answer the question with logic, you should be able to pass what the employer is testing.

Ok great, so now you know how to handle these stressful situations. What you probably want to know next is what types of questions may be asked of you by employers. Here is where the real fun begins. Employers have many tricks up their sleeves and it is your job to put them in their place (Politely of course). After this crash course on answering trick questions, not only will you be able to give them the answer they are looking for, but you may actually be able to teach them something that they didn't know. We will now begin to discuss some examples of what questions could be asked so that you can begin to become familiar with trick questions. Some of these examples I am providing here are the exact questions friends of mine, myself and past professors of mine have encountered in interviews throughout our careers. These questions have been asked by some of the largest companies worldwide throughout all genres of corporate positions. Let's now take a look at some real life examples. Some of the following examples are actually "trick questions" and other are just to test one's knowledge of using basic mathematics to calculate numbers in your head.

First let's start with the basics. You are in a first round interview. You have been asked several questions about your previous work experience and how you have demonstrated yourself as a leader. Great! You are doing an excellent job so far. Now, out of the blue, you are asked, *"Why are manhole covers round?"* Remember this may seem obscure but what you need to do is relax and think of a logical explanation. This question has been asked by numerous employers over the years. Hopefully you can think out the logical answer to this question. Think about it in geometric terms. The answer to why manhole covers are round is simply, so that they will not fall in. Think about it. If you took a square or rectangle sewer plate and turned it on its side (diagonally), it would fall right in. A union worker who is working in the sewer could get severely hurt if an individual were to drop that plate down the hole and onto someone's head. This is why manhole covers are indeed round. Again, think geometrically. You can not fit a circle inside a circle of the same size no matter what angle you turn it on.

See you did it! That wasn't so painful (except for the union worker who gets hit with a square manhole cover). If you really want to impress the employer, you can also inform him that an equilateral triangle would be the only other shape which could possibly give the same effect as a round manhole cover because it also would not be able to fall through. However, that would be one weird looking manhole cover. Wouldn't you agree? Now you have not only answered this question, but you explained your thought process to answering it and gave him extra information he/she didn't even ask for. There is a good chance the employer didn't even know previously that equilateral triangles could serve the purpose of a manhole cover. In this case, you know you have nailed this trick question.

Many of these types of questions are more modern based questions which started in the mid and late 90s during the tech-boom. Companies such as Google and Microsoft would ask their employees these types of questions. Bill Gates himself has even openly admitted to asking these types of questions. Mr. Gates has also been famous for asking questions such as, *"How would you move Mount Fuji?"* One fellow who worked for Microsoft actually was asked this on his interview with Bill Gates and decided to write a book on it and his experiences working at Microsoft. He included that exact question as the title of his book. Just like most trick questions asked by employers, there was no real answer to his question. Gates explained that he would have accepted quite a few answers to this question, however the main goal was to observe one's thought process and quick thinking techniques. If you are curious, some of the examples he did accept were Photoshop Mount Fuji or make a mathematical calculation on how to move the mountain. The rational is an employer wants to see its candidates be able to think outside the box. You will find that even some of the most intelligent people have the most difficulty answering these types of questions. It is important to remember that the employer is not always the most impressed by an individual's G.P.A. or standardized test scores. Often an employer wants to see if an employee can figure out a real life problem or calculation making logical reasoning.

These next few examples will be a bit more quantitative. Remember when you expressed to the employer that you have good quantitative skills? Now the employer is going to want you to prove it. Here is your chance to prove to him/her you possess these types of skills. Remember, these questions are not going to be hard. They are only hard if you make them hard for yourself. Rarely will you be asked to calculate a problem which requires a calculator. Think logically and you will be fine.

One time in an interview at a world-wide financial firm I was asked by the employer, *"If our company's NJ headquarters has 500,000 clients served by 250 advisers, what is the client/adviser ratio?"* The answer is simply 2,000:1. How did I arrive at the answer with no paper, pens or calculators? There are two ways you can solve this problem easily off the top of your head. How I would solve this problem would be to remember that 250 goes into 1000 exactly 4 times. Take the number 4 and multiply it by 500 which gives you 2,000. 2,000:1 is the correct client/adviser ratio the employer is looking for. Another way you can solve this problem would be to cancel the zeros in the numbers. Change the number 500,000 to 50,000 and 250 to 25. Now you need to divide 50,000 by 25. This is basic math. Again this gives you an answer of 2,000 or a client/adviser ratio of 2,000:1.

Sometimes the answers to the questions an employer will ask you are very simple, however the solution may have been an answer which you have never thought of before. There are some tricks in mathematics which often can catch you off guard. These types of questions are not tricks in reality, however an employer may position the question to you in a manner which may seem like a trick question. An interviewer for example may ask you a question such as this, *"If you have a client who invests $100,000 in the stock market and the market declines 20% this year. How much would the market need to appreciate next year to retain his full principal of $100,000?"* Almost all candidates think for a minute and respond with a confident tone that the answer is 20%. This is incorrect. Think! If you had $100,000 which you invested in the stock market this year and the market declines 20% which leaves you with $80,000 remaining, it would actually take a 25% increase in the market next year to retain your principal of $100,000. A 20% increase on $80,000 is only $96,000, which means you would need a significantly higher rate of appreciation next year than its rate of depreciation this year in order to retain your original principal. Always be cautious responding to an answer like this which seems too obvious.

Here is another question for you. Let's say you are on an interview and asked, *"How many quarters, stacked on edge, would it take to reach the top of the Empire State Building?"* Again relax, take a deep breath, and think. Not many people could give you the exact height of the empire state building if you asked them. The employer doesn't care if you are one of those people who do know the exact answer either, however, he does care if you are going to make an attempt to solve the problem. For your information the Empire State Building's height to its roof top is 1,250 feet high. Let's try and use round numbers and tell an employer that we think it is approximately 1,000 feet tall. (He will not correct you I promise.) A quarter is approximately one inch in diameter. There are 12 inches in a foot. This means that if a quarter is one inch in diameter, it will take 12 quarters to make up a foot in length. Now take the 12 quarters in a foot and multiply it by the 1,000 feet tall building. 12 times 1,000 equals 12,000. Your answer is 12,000. State to your employer with confidence that is would take 12,000 quarters stacked on edge to reach the top of the Empire State Building.

Breakdown:

Empire State Building = 1,000 feet tall
A quarter = 1" in diameter
12 quarters = 1 foot
12,000 quarters = 1,000 feet
Answer: **12,000 quarters**

Here is another problem similar to our last example. You are on an interview with an employer who is a graduate of Temple University. He explains that his daughter attends Gwynedd Mercy College in Montgomery County, PA and wants to drive from her school to Temple University located in North Philadelphia. He holds up a paper clip and asks you, *"How many of these paper clips lined up in a row would it take to reach Temple University from Gwynedd Mercy College?"* In the same fashion as the Empire State Building example, always pick numbers you can calculate in your head first. If you choose simple numbers, the problems will seem simple. However, if you pick hard numbers, the answer will seem like a nightmare to calculate. Start again with the size of the paper clip. Estimate a paper clip to be one inch. Is it really? Who knows, but who really cares anyway. It is always easy to multiply by one. Again you would have one paper clip for every inch in length. This means it would give you 12 paper clips for each foot because you have 12 inches in one foot. Temple University is approximately 18 miles away so let us just guess and say its 20 miles for round figures. There are 5,280 feet in one mile. Now we can take our 5,280 feet/mile and multiply it by 12 because there are 12 paper clips in one foot. To make it easy on yourself you need to use math tricks in your head. Take the 5,280 and multiple it by 10 which gives you 52,800. Take the 5,280 and multiply it by the remaining 2 which gives you 10,560. 52,800 plus 10,560 equals 63,360. Now take 63,360 and multiply it by 20. Tip: Whenever you can use the numbers 1 or 10 to multiply by, take advantage of it. When I chose 20 miles I was setting myself up for this part of the problem. Take 63,360 and multiply it by 10 miles which gives you 633,600. Then take the remaining 63,360 and multiply it by the other 10 miles which also gives you 633,600. The sum of 633,600 and 633,600 gives you a grand total of 1,267,200. Your answer to the employer is that is would take 1,267,200 paper clips lined up in a row to connect Gwynedd Mercy College to Temple University. If you have followed me so far you are doing well. I have two more examples for you which become a bit more challenging. Remember the key is to keep the numbers which you choose simple and you will be able to easily solve the problem.

Breakdown:

Paper clip = 1" in length
12 paper clips = 1 foot
Distance between schools = 20 miles
5,280 feet = 1 mile
12 paper clips/foot x 5,280 feet (5,280 x 10 = 52,800 and 5,280 x 2 = 10,560)
(52,800 + 10,560 = 63,360 paper clips/mile)
63,360 paper clips/mile x 20 miles (63,360 x 10 = 633,600 and 63,360 x 10 = 633,600) (633,600 + 633,600 = 1,267,200 total paper clips)
Answer: 1,267,200 paper clips

This next question has been commonly asked by multiple financial firms. It will baffle almost every candidate except the people who are reading this book. Not only will you be well prepared for these types of questions now, but you will also be able to answer them with confidence. The next example is after you have been discussing your future career goals and why you are choosing the firm you are interviewing with for a possible job opportunity. They then change gears and ask you, *"How many golf balls would be needed to fill the fuselage of a Boeing 767 aircraft?"* When you receive a question such as this you always need to make several assumptions if you wish to solve the problem. When you make these assumptions always remember to make the assumptions numerically in your favor so that you can make the calculations in your head. Sometimes the employer will tell you that you can use a pen and paper. In these rare cases then you can be more precise with your numbers and assumptions. However, in more cases than not he/she will expect you to make the calculations in your head. This is why you will keep your numbers simple. So how many golf balls can really be fit in a fuselage of a Boeing 767? This may indeed be a more difficult question than our previous questions, however it is still not as hard as you think. Let's start to solve it. First, we need to make our assumptions. Let's estimate that the fuselage is approximately 150 feet long and 20 feet in diameter. The golf balls are approximately one inch in diameter. We will also need to take into account the formula for volume of a container which equals height multiplied by area of base. You would then take the 20 foot diameter which creates a 10 foot radius. Remember the formula for Area? Area = Π *

r^2. Π=3.14 however 3.14 will be a difficult number to multiply in your head so we will round it to 3. Plug in your numbers. Area = 3*10^2. 10 squared gives you 100 and when you multiply it by round pie of 3 it gives you 300 square feet. Now you would take the area of 300 square feet and multiply it by the height of 150 feet. 300 square feet multiplied by 150 feet will give 45,000 cubic square feet. We can round that up to 50,000 so that we can more easily be able to make the calculation in our head. Make sure you inform the employer of this assumption along with all of your previous assumptions. Now that we have calculated cubic square feet, take your 1 inch in diameter golf ball, which would include 12 golf balls for each foot in length, and multiply it by the 12 inches in a foot three times. 1 multiplied by 12 by 12 gives you a face foot value of 144 balls. Now take the 144 balls and multiply it by 12 for a third and final time. 144 multiplied by 12 may be difficult to calculate in your head so take 144 and 10 which would give you 1,440. Take 144 times 2 which give you 288. Now add 1,440 and 288 together and it gives you just over 1,700 balls per cubic foot. Now take your original 50,000 cubic square feet and multiply it by the 1,700 balls per cubic foot and you have your final answer of 85 million. 85 million should be adjusted approximately 10% less because we previously had overstated the 45,000 cubic feet by 10% when we rounded it to 50,000. This means we have to take into account 90% of the total number to become as accurate as possible to the correct answer. 90% of the 85 million gives you an after adjustment total of 76.5 million golf balls. This is your final answer. You will then state approximately 76.5 million golf balls could be fit in the fuselage of a Boeing 767 aircraft. It may have taken you 10 minutes or so but you have just shocked the interviewer by answering such a question. It may still seem difficult to answer and calculate in your head but if you can practice these types of questions and understand the logic behind them, next time you are on an interview and a trick question is asked you will find yourself well prepared to answer such a question. These types of questions often seem a lot more difficult than they are in reality. The toughest part to answering these questions is doing basic math in your head while remaining calm. If this problem still seems a bit confusing I would recommend re-reading the material until it becomes familiar. The most confusing part of this problem may be only that you have forgotten simple mathematical equations. If you can remember the formulas for area and volume, this should be a rather simple calculation. We will try one final example before we conclude this chapter. Then I believe you will be well prepared to handle any type of trick question an employer asks you.

Breakdown:

Fuselage = 150 feet long
Fuselage = 20 feet in diameter
Golf ball = 1" diameter
Volume of container = height x area of base
Area = $\Pi * r^2$. $\Pi = 3.14$
20 foot diameter/2 = 10 foot radius
Base Area = 3.0 x 100 = 300 square feet
300 square feet x 150 feet = 45,000 cubic feet (take 50,000 cubic feet)
1" x 12" x 12 = 144 balls in a face foot (remember that 12 inches are in 1 foot to solve)
144 x 12 = 1,440 + 288 = 1,700 golf balls/cubic foot

(It is always easier to use tricks such as these to help yourself by taking multiples of ten to multiply. Then use the remaining number, in this case 2, and multiply it by 144. Lastly, add your two totals together which gives you your estimated answer for the problem's last step.)

50,000 cubic feet x 1,700 balls/cubic foot = 85 million
Adjust: 85 million-(10% x 85 million) = 76.5 million golf balls
Answer: 76.5 million golf balls

Finally, this last question came from a friend I had, whom for four years had always talked about this one company which was his "dream company" to work for. Finally after 3 ½ years of college he receives a call from them explaining to him that they have received his resume and wanted to set up an interview with him. Nervous and overjoyed he came to me and one of the professors at our university asking for advice. We had known in advance that this particular employer was known for asking in depth quantitative questions along with trick questions as well. We also had heard of one question that they commonly asked its candidates to solve. The question they liked to commonly ask was, *"Estimate for me the market for disposable diapers in China."* A normal candidate would be looking at the employer with a look as if he is really serious. You on the other hand should be ready to start calculating numbers and giving him an educated answer while explaining your theory out loud. Again we need to make assumptions before we start making any calculations. We can first agree that China has approximately a population of 1.2 billion people.

However 1.2 billion may be a difficult number to multiply off the top of your head so let's adjust the number to 1 billion for now. Of the 1 billion, approximately 50% are men and 50% are women. Half of 1 billion is 500 million which gives us our female population. Of the 500 million women in China, 20% are of childbearing age, which leaves us with 100 million women. Of these 100 million, approximately 10% actually have children each year which leaves us with 10 million women giving birth to infants. Each infant averages use of 4 diapers per day. 4 diapers each day for 365 days in a year gives you about 1,400 diapers a year per infant. 1,400 diapers per infant annually multiplied by 10 million infants interprets to 14 billion diapers. If there is a 10% market share for the 14 billion diapers which would give you a total of 1.4 billion diapers per year. We are almost finished! Remember how we only calculated 1 billion of 1.2 billion China citizens so that we could more easily make the calculation? We should now make 20% adjustment for this variance. 1.4 billion multiplied by 1.20 would then give you just under 1.7 billion diapers. 1.7 billion diapers would be your final answer. Now that's a lot of s***! A little trickier than the previous examples, but it is still not too hard. We then practiced this China disposable diaper rate example repeatedly for a good hour until he mastered the question.

Breakdown:

1.2 billion population (Adjust to 1.0)
Half female/half male = 500 million
20% of childbearing age = 100 million
10% have children each year = 10 million
Average of 4 diapers per day in a 365 day year = approx. 1,400 diapers per baby/year
1,400 diapers x 10 million infants = 14 billion diapers
10% market share = 1.4 billion diapers/year
20% calculation adjustment (1.0 billion to 1.2 billion population) = 1.7 billion diapers/year
Answer: 1.7 billion diapers/year

Finally the day of the interview was here. My friend was seated for the interview while being asked a variety of numerous questions. When he came home that night he said, "Mike, they didn't ask me that question after all that." I then replied, "They didn't?" He said, "No, but they did ask me to *Estimate the market for disposable diapers in the USA!*" My friend said, "But I did ace the question and I got the job!" I congratulated him because I knew even though he did not get the exact question, that I had still prepared him well for the question. The calculation was nearly the same. He only had to change 2 numbers in the entire problem. The United States population and market share had to be different. In the interview, instead of taking a population of 1.2 billion, we now needed to change that starting population number to 300 million which is the United States estimated population. Again, assume half of the population are women which gives you 150 million. Of those 150 million women, 20% are of childbearing age which leaves us with 30 million women. 10% of those 30 million women have children each year which now leaves us with 3 million women having babies each year. Again assume 4 diapers are used each day by infants for 365 days in a year which is approximately 1,400 diapers. Now take the 3 million women who are giving birth to babies this year and multiply it by 1,400 diapers used by each infant annually which will total to 4.2 billion diapers. Of the 4.2 billion diapers, there is a market share of 75% which leaves you with just over 3 billion diapers each year. My friend told the employers that the final answer is 3 billion diapers annually. Not only did my friend answer the question correctly, the employer was beyond impressed and had informed my friend that he had given the best response to the question among every candidate he had ever interviewed. My friend was then offered the position for the company.

Breakdown:

300 million population
Half female/half male = 150 million
20% of childbearing age = 30 million
10% have children each year = 3 million
Average of 4 diapers per day in a 365 day year = approx. 1,400 diapers per baby/year
1,400 diapers x 3 million infants = 4.2 billion diapers
75% market share = 3 billion diapers/year
Answer: 3 billion diapers/year

Often employers will ask bizarre questions such as these to see how you react and think under pressure. If you remain calm and make an attempt to solve the problem, this part of the interview shouldn't hurt you. If anything this may win you the position with the person interviewing you. Don't worry about making every single calculation precise. If you go back through these problems which we have discussed again, you will notice I used a significant amount of rounded numbers. This is quite alright if you can explain your reasoning out loud to the employer interviewing you. These types of questions can be as easy or hard as you wish to make them. If you are smart you will always use round number and ones that you can easily calculate in you head. I am certain you are an intelligent student if you are picking up this book on your own free time so that you can better your own career.

In the next and final chapter, we will wrap up the key points on how to obtain your dream internship or job. I will also include topics that you may use in conversations with employers and things you shouldn't discuss. Many of these point may seem obvious and other may not. Throughout my experiences I have found that it is important to make someone aware of all situations when in doubt. These topics will be discussed in more detail in our final chapter.

CHAPTER 8

"To Say or Not to Say? That is the Question."

It is important to distinguish the difference between which topics are appropriate for discussion in the place of work from the things that should be left for conversations on your personal time. Many of the topics we will discuss in this chapter may seem obvious, however many employees do not take the hint. I have mastered this discipline throughout personal experiences over my career with other co-ops and co-workers. Referring back to earlier in the book, whenever in doubt take the most conservative approach to the situation. You never can fully know how each person will react to a comment.

There are a few categories I would completely stay away from discussing in the work place. You may use the R.A.P. rule to help you remember these three categories. R.A.P. is an acronym I have created which stands for religion, after-work reckless activities, and politics. In almost all scenarios, it is best if you avoid discussing these topics with your boss and co-workers. Each of these subjects can be very touchy where each person has different views and beliefs on the same issue. It is near impossible to find a situation where one of these topics is discussed and every individual agrees on the same point. This is why it should be avoided at all cost. For example, you and your boss have got along excellent for the three years that you have been working for him. One day you meet him in the office kitchenette for coffee and say, "Have you seen the news? George Bush has really lost control over this country. He has wasted so much in this unnecessary war in Iraq. What an idiot. There goes our social security money." All of a sudden your boss fires back, "I don't agree with that. Our president is trying to maintain homeland security and do what is best for Americans' safety." The debate becomes more intense between the two until both of you decide to part ways in an awkward silence. A week passes and you assume everything is back to normal. You remind your boss about that promotion he was talking to you about and he then responds to you with an answer which doesn't seem too promising that the position is still available. Is this fair? Maybe it is and maybe it isn't. This is why it is just good advice to avoid these types of conversations at all cost. I can assure you that these conversations will never work to your benefit. Because you had this political discussion with your boss, it may have very well eliminated your chances of obtaining the promotion you have hoped for the last six months.

The first letter in R.A.P. stands for religion. Religion is a wonderful thing and it is the foundation for the values and beliefs which the majority of Americans and people across the world live their lives. Religion is alright to talk about if you are talking in terms such as if you make statements like "I went to mass this past weekend" or "I can't wait to celebrate Christmas vacation with my family this year." These types of expressions are fine to make. The type of religious statements you want to stay away from are statements which get into the history of one religion versus another, and what major beliefs are most likely true. Also abortion can be a religious discussed issue. Regardless what your stance and beliefs are on abortion, this is a topic you especially want to leave out of discussion in the work place. This is true for a situation where others are discussing the issue first and you are asked by others, "What is your stance on abortion?" Even if they ask you, you should respond with a polite answer and state that you really rather not comment, you don't feel strongly one way or another, or even just simply that you do not have a strong knowledge of the subject. All of these types of responses are certainly acceptable and it will avoid awkward confrontation at all costs.

Next, after-work reckless activities should also be avoided for at work discussions. If you want to discuss a work happy hour or a party you went to where you had one or two beers that is certainly fine. What you want to stay away from is discussing that you were drunk beyond believe during the weekend. Hopefully you do not participate in any major reckless behavior, however if this may occur, do not share your weekend stories with the entire office. The story may not cost you your job, however it just doesn't look professional and it certainly may hurt your chances of obtaining a promotion within the company. How can you represent and be the C.E.O. of the company when everyone who works for you remembers the days when you got drunk every Friday at the work happy hours?

There is a time and a place for everything. No one ever said you can't go out and have a good time on the weekends, however, always remember where you are when you are discussing these stories. Also, if you unfortunately have ever been convicted of a felony or had been arrested, this would be another thing which should not be disclosed among your co-workers. Never lie on your application about it if you have been convicted of a felony, however if the employer still decides to hire you regardless of your criminal record, you should then no longer bring this topic of conversation up among your fellow co-workers. This is confidential information between you and your employer and is unnecessary to be shared with your entire staff. Always use your best judgment in these types of situations.

The last part of the acronym R.A.P. is politics. This is often America's most heated debate of them all. This should already be a strong indicant that these types of discussions are best omitted from conversation in the work place. In the beginning of this chapter I have already given an example of how politics can influence your performance rating and how people feel about you regard-less whether or not it is relevant to your accomplishments and achievements. It is important to remain open to all opinions in any discussion, however, politics is one of the few topics which closes the door for acceptance of new opinions and complete collaboration of ideas for one common goal. It would be nice it this were possible. The world would be a lot simpler place, however this is not the reality of the subject matter. Therefore not discussing politics in the work place would be the most conservative and best approach.

What should be discussed and what should not be discussed will typically be common sense for most people to decipher, however if ever in doubt it would be the best approach from refraining from stating it. I believe this book has given you great insight for mastering the art of professionalism. I am confi-dent you are now ready to obtain your first internship or job. My goal for this book was to enhance the professional development of individuals who are in the early stages of their career, searching for an entry level position in their field of study. I feel that I have accomplished this goal.

Besides the topics which fall under RAP, the last thing I want to discuss in this book is the internet and their exposure to the public. If I could give college kids one last word of advice in our modern day society, it would be to be very cautious of their use of technology and the internet. This includes being very cautious of what you and your friends post about your personal life on the internet for anyone in the general public to see. Employers may base their decisions on whether to hire you based on pictures you appear in and blogs which you have written. Is it fair for an employer to judge you based on your online pictures? The answer is probably not, assuming you are qualified for the position. However, the reality is that employers ultimately make predetermined decisions based on first impressions and how they view a person outside of the work place.

Websites such as Facebook and MySpace have certainly been revolutionary changes in our society today. I am not so sure if these changes are for the best, but they certainly have changed the society we live in today. It is great how Facebook and MySpace has allowed us to express ourselves to others, share interests, and meet people, however it also has created an open door for professional contacts to observe your weekend activities. My advice to college students would be to be very careful what they post of themselves on the internet. I am not saying do not open a Facebook or MySpace account either, but think about what you post about yourself on the internet before doing so. Whenever you are in doubt, I would advise refraining from posting it on the internet and into the hands of the general public.

There are many things about these sites such as Facebook and MySpace which college kids do not realize. These sites have options where they can hide themselves from being included in searches and block themselves from others viewing their page. It is true these options do exist, however believe me when I say that I have heard of employers who have found ways to access these pages despite the block or hide options which exist. Employers have even created fake accounts and requested applicants as their friends. If the applicant was gullible enough to fall into their trap in anticipation of making a new friend, their block option had no real purpose after all. Be careful who you select and accept as your friends on these sites. Often, it may be possible that the employer has a current employee who you are friends with and has a Facebook account. The employer may then observe your page from his employee's account. There is even the extreme case where an employer pays a skilled computer technician to hack into these sites. I am not sure if that technique is even legal and it is probably an extremely rare case, however it is a possibility. The beauty pageant winner, Miss New Jersey, was even humiliated and possibly hurt in her chances to become Miss America due to pictures she has posted on the internet from her days in college.

If you are the type of college student who still has the urge to post pictures of your weekend insanity, at least have the intelligence to not use you real name when you create your online account. I am not condoning this type of behavior to begin with, but I am trying to make a valid and rational point. The bottom line is these types of pictures and descriptions of yourself does not belong on the internet for the entire world to see. If you take my advice and use common sense in these types of situations you will be much more respected in the eyes of the pubic.

No one ever fully knows what their future endeavors are and what past actions and evidence could hurt their future career performance. This is the reason it is so crucial to get into the habit of eliminating any misconceptions in the eyes of the public. Politics is notorious for having this reputation of a public figure being wrongly depicted based on previous actions from their youth. The internet in our society today makes it that much easier to ruin one's reputation based upon one bad decision or misconception.

The moral of the internet story is, if you post something you wouldn't want an employer to see, don't post it on the internet. Always keep the mentality that there is always the possibility they could access your webpage. Remember this next time you hear of your friend or someone you meet explain they were not hired because of a Facebook picture, with two keg taps in his mouth, seen by an employer. Again, it may not be fair but an employer may associate irresponsibility outside the workplace to irresponsibility in the workplace.

During the final process of writing this book I sampled hundreds of local college students at random and asked them a series of four questions and the results were extremely surprising to me. In my opinion, the percentage of internship participation was quite low. The four questions, which I asked each college student, were the following:

As a college student have you ever thought about doing an internship?

Have you built a resume in order to apply for internships?

As a student do you know how or where to apply for internships?

Have you participated in an internship?

93% of the students I surveyed said they had at least thought of participating in an internship regardless if they have actually done one or not. 63% of the students said they have at least created a resume at some point during their college years. This next stat is shocking and is in desperate need of improvement. Only 40% of college students said they even know where to start looking to obtain an internship. Finally, 37% of students said they had actually participated in an internship. Even though 37% is still an extremely low percentage, it is positive that the ratio between students who knew where to search for internships and students who have actually done an internship was a relatively small variance. As a side note, several students expressed to me that they were still not able to participate in the internships they most desired. *The Professional Code of Conduct* hopefully has helped you with these types of problems. If this book in anyway could impact these statistics positively, then this book has been a definite success. If you felt this book has help you significantly in your career or feel the information in this book was valuable, I would appreciate it if you could spread the word on to at least three other people you know who you feel it could impact. As college students, we still have great room for improvement in the pursuit of obtaining internships and corporate world experience before actually graduating.

When applying for internships and jobs as a college student, always take advantage of the student professional development centers first. These centers, which are almost always free with your tuition, will help you develop your resume if you are unsure how to create one and help you find your first internship which you have been trying to obtain. It is to your own advantage to use these centers effectively because they will help you become more marketable to employers and make it convenient for you to meet with employers. If you are unsure where these centers are located, check the school's website or ask other college students if needed. It is important to ask questions. Your career depends on it. Even though it is a rarity, some schools may not offer these centers and if so then it is important to search the internet for internship postings or even pick up the newspaper and search in the job listing sections. The internet is a great tool which has impacted many things in our society, especially the job search process. There are several websites I would recommend which are advertised on television. CareerBuilder.com, Monster.com, HotJobs.com, JobSearchUSA.org and many others are great sources which are free websites where you can post your resume, update your resume and apply to jobs specific to the industry of your choice. I would strongly recommend taking advantage of such resources, which lie at your fingertips from your own personal P.C. in your home or dorm room.

Let's recap the important topics of this book before we conclude. Always remember when building a resume and interviewing with employers that you need to be the solution to their problem. Ask yourself before taking any of these steps, how can I prove to an employer that I can add value to their firm? Remember to include the 4 major skills of communications, leadership, teamwork and quantitative analysis. Be prepared at all times to give specific examples of each and how you have proven that you demonstrated these skills in real life situations.

Don't wait until the last moment. Apply to internships and co-ops early in your college career so that you can obtain your dream job directly out of college. Always act and dress professional. Whenever in doubt, business professional is the only attitude and wardrobe which should be carried with you into the interview. Use the rule of conservatism throughout your career.

Finally, when networking and interviewing with employers remain calm. You now have all the tools needed to be successful. Make use of these tools and express your skills which you possess to an employer. It is your time to shine, so make the best of it. As your career progresses and you interview more, this nervousness will lessen and you will become more and more comfortable selling yourself to others. Experience reduces nerves when speaking with others, this is why the importance of gaining the experience early in your career is so crucial and heavily stressed in this book.

I thank you for taking the time to read this book. I can assure you that you are now much more ahead of most college students' career progress just for reading this book. Remember, in most cases you already have all the tools and skills the employer is looking for in its candidate. You just need to develop these skills and prove to an employer you possess them. Take my advice and I can assure you that you will be glad with the progression of your career. I want to wish you the best of luck with your future endeavors. Feedback is always greatly appreciated. If you have any questions or recommendations for improvement please do not hesitate to contact me at MikeBottaro@aol.com. Feedback is one of the best ways for us to learn and make corrections to our own work in our careers. Thank you again. Good luck in that new position which you will be holding shortly. This is indeed the proper guideline to the professional code of conduct which hopefully each of you will live by so that you can strive to maximize your professional talents and soar to the top of the corporate ladder in your career.

978-0-595-46890-4
0-595-46890-X